Praise

'This book challenges the status quo about ageing and wellbeing. It is both personal and informative, touching on every little aspect that affects us physically, emotionally and socially, without being too "medical" and difficult to read. After reading this book, you will feel empowered to change your life for the better.'

— Melanie Benham, patient

'This book is incredible – a reflective, cutting-edge resource for those wanting to revitalise their face and body sustainably. Every woman needs to read this book.'

— Dr Shah-Desai,
aesthetic oculoplastic surgeon

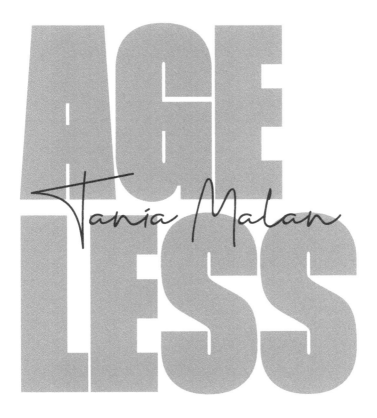

AGE LESS

Tania Malan

The cellular secrets to
looking and feeling your best

R^ethink

First published in Great Britain in 2022 by
Rethink Press (www.rethinkpress.com)

Disclaimer
The advice in this book should not replace proper medical advice from your doctor. It should not serve as medical advice or any form of medical treatment. Please always speak to your doctor before changing any of your medical treatments. This book has been written and published for informational and educational purposes only, so please use it as informational only and not as a substitute for individual or medical care.

This book is dedicated to people everywhere. We are all on the journey of life, a journey which changes us at a cellular level, affecting our health and wellbeing. No matter your age, you matter.

Contents

Foreword

As a UK-based aesthetic oculoplastic surgeon attracting patients globally for my trademarked eye and face rejuvenating procedures, I am constantly surrounded by those seeking the 'holy grail' of aesthetics. Over the course of my career I have come to realise that the physical signs of ageing in my patients' faces are not primarily due to their genetics (despite their complaints to the contrary) but are instead compounded by the impact of stress and lifestyle. Like so many busy surgeons, I live the dream by hanging on tight to the runaway train of 'successful modern life': wife, parent, child, academic, researcher, educator and business owner. A heightened awareness of my own accelerated ageing (fuelled by a love of chocolate and by menopausal hormonal decline) triggered a pursuit for the missing pieces of the aesthetic jigsaw.

I had the pleasure of meeting Tania Malan as a delegate on one of my cadaveric facial anatomy courses. Her intense curiosity and intelligence impressed me instantly and led to us engaging in a more meaningful conversation over lunch. In direct opposition to the media portrayal of the 'aesthetic boom' as a vanity-driven industry whose sole purpose is the denial and rejection of nature, our professional (and personal) quests had evolved from simple anti-ageing treatments into a bigger question: How could we combine these treatments with tapping into our genes to optimise health and age well?

Most of our patients wanted instant gratification. They would present three or four times a year to 'fix' the outside while ignoring the inside. Tania had noticed that when they started using DNA testing to optimise their nutrition, hormones and lifestyle choices, the results were nothing short of spectacular. It was almost as if they were travelling back in time.

I am delighted that Tania's aesthetic journey over the last thirty years has inspired her to put pen to paper, encapsulating the complex issue of ageing in such a relevant, evidence-based and holistic manner. I am also honoured that Tania invited me to write the foreword to her incredible book – a reflective, cutting-edge resource for those wanting to revitalise their face and body sustainably.

I highly recommend *Ageless* to medical professionals and patients alike. After reading it you will, like me, feel empowered to change your life for the better. Press the pause button and age less.

Dr Sabrina Shah-Desai MS, FRCS (Ed) Ophth

Aesthetic Oculoplastic Surgeon
Visiting Prof Anatomy, University of Camerino, Italy

Medical Director, Perfect Eyes Ltd
Director, Oculo-Facial Aesthetic Academy (OFAA)

Founder, Dr Sabrina Dark Circle Corrector System

🌐 www.perfecteyesltd.com
📷 @drsabrinashahdesai

Introduction

Suzanne settles onto the couch with a look of both trepidation and anticipation. She seems vulnerable and uncomfortable as I invite her to tell me why she's here. The words spill out and, like every other patient attending my clinic, she tells a story of superficial concerns about her face while her hand unconsciously touches the troublesome areas. She wants Botox and fillers, but she's unsure exactly what she needs.

I keep listening until she finally goes quiet, with the familiar look of dread. I acknowledge her concerns, then ask the most crucial question: 'What happened?' I can hear the gears shifting in her head. She shuffles uneasily, facing her reality and the pain associated with it. The tears well up as the deeper story bubbles to the surface. Now we can start getting to the truth.

I have interviewed over 500 women, and invariably I hear the same story: 'There's a mismatch between how I feel and how I look. I look tired and old, but on the inside I still feel about thirty. I have hooded eyes; my skin is sagging and my make-up doesn't go on as it used to. People say I look sad when I'm not or that I have a "resting bitch face". I look in the mirror and do a double take. Is that me? I look more like my mother. I wish I'd looked after myself and my skin better. I don't know what it is to feel and look like me anymore. I constantly ache, I don't sleep well and I have continual night sweats. I have brain fog, I'm forgetful and tired all the time. I feel low and have no confidence. I hate having my photo taken. Sex used to be the highlight of my weekend; now I'm not interested. I don't want to look young; I just want to look better for my age.'

As we reach our second act, at around forty-five, our body is changing both inwardly and outwardly. Our hormones are all over the place, wreaking havoc with our mind, memory, libido, bones, tissues, skin – the list goes on. Suddenly everything about ourself bothers us, our confidence falters and we feel old, insecure, not ourself. The light goes out of our eyes and our head hangs a little lower. Our wellbeing is in jeopardy. When did this happen? How? Why? What can we do about it?

My clients tell me they have repeatedly seen their GP, who cannot find anything wrong. They are scared of having cosmetic treatment, because they don't know whom to trust and they don't want to end up with a 'trout pout'. They don't want people to know that they have had work done; they want to look 'natural'. They also feel guilty about spending money on themselves.

It is an assumed fact of life that we all age. Increasingly, though, ageing is being seen as a disease,[1] with specific causes, recognisable signs and symptoms, and effects at a cellular and molecular level.[2] Ageing is one of the leading causes of suffering because it impacts our bodies from a molecular level to our cells, organs, muscle and bone.[3] Everyone feels the effects of ageing at some stage, whether it is aching joints, physical pain, tiredness, lack of energy or chronic disease. We all try to beat ageing: by doing exercise, eating more healthily, resting more, sleeping better or improving our wellbeing – a process known as 'biohacking'.

Some of us go further by undergoing cosmetic surgery or its less invasive alternative, aesthetic medicine, which aims to enhance and improve our appearance through minimally invasive nonsurgical treatments. These treatments include Botox, dermal fillers and skincare. Recent advances in technology and personalised medicine have led to an explosion of available products and treatments, but there are two huge problems in the market.

The first problem is that we are overwhelmed and confused by the number of options available to us, and by the significant disparity in costs and promised benefits. The second is that the majority of products and treatments focus on the outside of the body, completely disregarding the inside, which is arguably where some of the most significant causes of ageing occur. The emphasis is on preventing chronic disease, on counteracting the changes caused by ageing, rather than on achieving agelessness. A healthy lifestyle, achieved through diet and exercise, used to be seen as the best way to fight ageing and boost wellbeing, but this is no longer the case. Rapid advances in technology and science are opening doors to the possibility of reversing ageing and extending lifespan.

What if we could be shown how to age less? Would that not be more proactive, more life-changing?

I am the founder of Uniskin Wellness Clinic. I am an advanced nurse practitioner with thirty years' experience in trauma and medicine in South Africa and the UK. My journey has taken a lot of meandering paths. In 1991 I qualified as a nurse in psychiatry, midwifery and community nursing, but my passion and interest lay in trauma medicine, where I practised in the early days of my career. One particular event made a significant impression on me and has continued to shape my practice to this day, as I will explain. I then worked in war-torn South Africa, learning to manage injury, illness, disease and wellbeing. Today I practise as a cosmetic and ageless specialist nurse and have treated over 300,000 people. I have four degrees, three at master's level, including an MSc in aesthetic medicine. I have written twenty-eight research papers and several training textbooks, and I am a visiting lecturer at various universities.

During my studies, I came across numerous documents that challenged accepted ideas about ageing, and they struck a chord deep with me. We are now living much longer but not necessarily better, and we are dying slowly and painfully. We need to overhaul our approach to ageing – not everything can be sorted with a tablet. We have been treating the consequences and not the cause. For a long time, I have subconsciously believed that we should and could do more. I have a passion for the human body and an unshakeable belief in its ability to heal itself. All it needs is better understanding and a hand from us.

I care about people and want to make humanity the best it can be. This drives me to study constantly – and drove me to write this book. My mission is to bring about real change for my patients by harnessing the technology and innovation around ageing. My approach is through personalised medicine, with the aim of reversing ageing and extending health span.

In *Ageless* I equip you with knowledge that reduces your uncertainty and vulnerability in a rapidly growing market where it is difficult to make an informed decision. I give you clear advice, showing you how to unlock your inner vitality and restore your confidence in your appearance. Above all, I help you to make better decisions – decisions that will improve your health and wellbeing. My thirty years in medicine have provided me with many case studies which I use to illustrate the issues and treatments I discuss. I have also developed unique models and strategies that will restore and rejuvenate you and empower you to live healthily for many years to come.

I believe ageing is a disease that, like other diseases, can be not only treated, but prevented. I explain why inadequate nutrition ages us and offer treatment solutions that will optimise your health and improve your wellbeing. I detail the anatomical changes that come with age and the impact these have on our facial features and skin. I consider the latest advances in nutrigenomics, using DNA for personalised, precision treatments to remove the guesswork during diagnosis. I also discuss the various treatments available and show you why and when they are needed. I examine and explain what is happening to you at the cellular level inwardly and outwardly and what you can do to age less.

The majority of cosmetic treatments focus on one particular element, which we are led to perceive as the root of our problems, but one treatment cannot solve an issue as complex as ageing. This book is unique in addressing the fundamental underlying problems and offering multiple and alternative solutions. You are a physical, emotional and social being – investigating and treating you as a whole will yield better outcomes than focusing on individual parts. Each area, such as your nutrition and hormones, contributes to how you feel and look.

In the following chapters, I show a tapestry of cause and effect that will give you a better understanding of the human body and its resilience. They are divided into three parts. In Part One I explain ageing, how our life events and surroundings – especially stress and injury – are contributory factors, and how our body responds to those impacts. Part Two is about diagnosing and bio-hacking your body, improving health outcomes using the latest innovations in medicine, such as your DNA, bioidentical hormones and supplements. In Part Three I describe the outward changes to our facial structure and skin and the aesthetic innovations designed to limit these and make us feel better about ourself.

The aim of agelessness is to facilitate a healthy and engaged old age and to support every individual in remaining powerful, fully actualised, and looking and feeling vital in an optimal state of wellbeing that doesn't put the onus on society to look after us. The better we look after our bodies with the knowledge we have, the better chance we have of living free from chronic disease.

Part One

HOW DAILY ASSAULTS ON OUR BODY CONTRIBUTE TO AGEING

This first part of the book presents ageing as a disease that can be slowed down or even prevented, challenging the notion that we should simply accept ageing and 'grow old gracefully'. Ageing is caused by the daily 'damage' we suffer as a result of our genetics, our lifestyles, our nutrition and our environment. Everyone experiences traumatic events in their lives. The context varies, but they almost always involve one or more of the following elements: loss, shock, injury or illness. Traumatic events can have a physical, social, emotional or financial impact. This impact causes a ripple effect at a cellular level, with repercussions that can be felt and seen immediately or later in life, affecting our wellbeing. Whatever the cause, the result is ageing. In the following chapters I will use a seminal case study to explain the links between life events and ageing – in particular, trauma, injury and pain, which accelerate ageing – and how the body responds to regulate and heal itself.

How Trauma Accelerates Cellular Ageing

Ageing is a complex molecular process driven by diverse pathways and biochemical events which are influenced by genetics and environmental factors, contributing to changes in our bodies. This exposure of our bodies to the onslaught of multiple events affects us at a cellular level. It is a multifaceted process, one event leading to another and each contributing to the entirety of our cellular being, and it results in a progressive functional decline in cells, tissues and organisms. Injury, illness, stress, anxiety, depression and menopause all contribute to disrupting the delicate balance within our bodies known as homeostasis. This results in sarcopenia (loss of muscle mass), telomere shortening, cell senescence, genome instability, mitochondrial dysfunction, epigenetic alterations and deregulation of nutrient sensing, leading to stem cell exhaustion and ageing.

To illustrate these effects, I will use the case of Mr H (not his real name), which deeply changed my life, my practice and my understanding of ageing.

The year was 1994, and it was a typical Saturday in our trauma unit in South Africa. It was heaving with the results of DIY mishaps, drunken fights and sports injuries, combined with the usual array of illnesses. It was all hands on deck. Then things suddenly got a lot worse. We received a call informing us that a thirty-eight-year-old male had been attacked by a crocodile and his right leg was partially severed and haemor-rhaging. He would be arriving in fifteen minutes.

When Mr H was wheeled in by the crew, it was a sight I will never forget. He was pale and sweaty, indicating that he had suffered shock and significant blood loss. We lifted the blankets off him to assess the damage and were met by a grotesque scene. His right leg was partially severed, his femur attached only by bits of tendon and tissue, with multiple bites visible on the bone and tissue. Strangely, there was very little blood (usually caused by shock and bleeding out), but there was a pervasive smell of blood, excrement and a 'darkness' that I later learned was typical of a crocodile attack – and which from that day on I would recognise anywhere. I clocked multiple other injuries, to his hands in particular, but I knew that our challenge was to keep him alive, so we quickly stabilised him and packed him off to theatre.

Maslow's Hierarchy of Needs

Maslow's Hierarchy of Needs forms the basis of nursing care.[4] It stems from motivational theory in psychology and comprises a five-tier model of human needs, divided into two categories: higher-order and lower-order needs. A need is something a person has to have to be healthy, and the urgency of needs varies between individuals. Each level must be met before a person can move up to the next one.

The most basic needs are on the lowest level and include food and shelter – physiological needs. The next level up is about safety and security, including financial. At the highest level is the need for self-actualisation – the urge to become what we are capable of being and the desire to be self-content. In aesthetic practice, patients also want to look pleasing to be self-actualised. In Mr H's case, this meant avoiding life-threatening sepsis by monitoring vital signs hourly and providing pain management, nourishment, rest and comfort.

The outward effects of trauma

The following day, I walked into the surgical ward to start my shift. Mr H was a mess. He was crying out in pain and fear and did not seem fully alert. His hair was oily and unwashed, clogged with soil and vomit. His skin was grey, as a result of blood loss, but also had that peculiar glow and smell caused by the adrenaline response that follows any trauma.

Most obvious and distressing of all was his stump. His right leg had been amputated mid-thigh and looked huge with the packed, soiled bandages. His wound had seeped blood during the night, as the stump wasn't closed off by the usual skin flap and had been left open, with the bone protruding, as an animal bite needs further debridement (cutting away of dead skin caused by infection) over several days.

As a result of this seepage, the room had a pervasive smell of rot caused by gas gangrene, a bacterial infection that produces gas within the tissues. This deadly form of gangrene, typical of a crocodile bite wound, is usually caused by clostridium perfringens bacteria. The bacteria were eating his flesh and his life was in the balance.

Over the following days, not only was Mr H subjected to daily general anaesthetics to enable the wound debridement but, because it had to be left open, he also had to continuously witness his horrific injury, which caused him severe emotional stress, or post-traumatic stress disorder. We all feel better when we have a plaster or a dressing on a wound and cannot see or feel the damage to our flesh.

The body's survival mechanism

Events such as injury, surgery, trauma and illness cause a stress response that results in changes in endocrine, metabolic and immunity function.[5] Stress hormones and cytokines play a role in these reactions, as I will explain later. The body's oxygen and energy requirements increase in proportion to the severity of the trauma. Greater reactions follow greater stress, ultimately leading to greater breakdown effects. Intensive breakdown reactions harm the body as they destroy muscle tissue and reduce energy storage, which prolongs recovery time and leads to ageing.

If we are to survive, we need energy. Cells throughout our body are highly tuned to energy information and achieve this through a mechanism known as nutrient and energy sensing. We obtain our energy from dietary intake in the form of nutrients. The nutrients are metabolised into fuel and other molecules, which power cellular processes. The typical response following a traumatic event is that the body starts to hypermetabolise, which means that it increases its energy expenditure, consuming more protein and fat, while protecting body fluid and electrolytes. Free fatty acids within our muscles are the primary sources of energy but only for a certain amount of time; then our bodies start on adipose (fat) tissue, skin and other surrounding tissues, eventually destroying them. Hypermetabolism leads to extreme weight loss. It is for these reasons that nutritional support is key.

Our skeletal muscle is the most significant contributor of energy, which it stores in pools ready for any event. The more muscle, the more energy. In stress, trauma and injury, the body shifts towards catabolism, or degradation, to provide energy to the most critical tissues, usually the brain, heart, liver and kidneys. Humans respond to stress in two places. The first is the sympathetic nervous system, where our heart rate, breathing, sweating, digestion and blood glucose increase in readiness for flight. The second is the blood, where increased circulation creates cortisol.

Cortisol is a chronic stress hormone released due to haemorrhage, infection, cold exposure, drop in blood sugar, exercise, trauma, toxins, emotions and pain.

These further degrade muscle protein to provide for the immune system, respond to infection, repair damaged tissue and provide energy. During constant stress our body inhibits other hormones to maintain the cortisol pathway as long as it is needed. Inhibiting the hormones pregnenolone and progesterone leads to worsening symptoms such as insomnia, anxiety and reduced immunity. The metabolic processes also cause high levels of toxicity known as oxidative damage.

The role of DNA in cellular renewal

Every function in our body is controlled by hormones, which are chemical messengers circulating in our bloodstream to prompt cells to maintain our natural state of equilibrium. One such pathway is cell growth and renewal. Every day, our bodies undergo a microscopic upheaval where 40 trillion cells die and need replacing. An excellent example of this is our skin, which consists of dead outer layers that require removing and replacing by fresh skin from beneath.

To begin with, the cells repeatedly divide to produce reserve cells, or stem cells. Stem cells are responsible for maintenance purposes and are stored in stem cell pools – little niches in various parts of our bodies – waiting for the call to repair. For stem cells to remain healthy and fresh, their environment needs to be healthy.

When cells are damaged, they either heal themselves or make new cells to replace those that are beyond repair. Badly damaged cells might kill themselves to make way for new ones. The less injured cells switch on genes to help with cell restoration and regeneration of tissue. They make copies of themselves to fill the gaps left when the others die. Even after the destruction of many cells, the surrounding cells can replicate themselves, quickly replacing the destroyed cells. The same process happens in wound healing as in the general maintenance of our body.

If a new cell replaces an old cell, it needs to have the same genetic code provided by our DNA. Each of the trillion cells in our bodies has two metres of DNA, which contains the information needed to build us. DNA provides every person with a 'handbook' that determines our molecular instructions for life: how we look and function, our traits and how we reproduce and grow. DNA ensures continuity from one generation to the next, but still allows for small changes that make us diverse. Our DNA splits into forty-six strings (twenty-three from each parent) known as chromosomes. At the end of each chromosome is a protective cap known as a telomere. Telomere shortening occurs at each DNA replication and, if repeated, leads to chromosomal degradation and cell death.

Telomere shortening

Telomeres are indicators of the health and history of a cell, providing a running report on the cell's condition. It is possible to test for telomeres through either a blood test or a DNA test called a TeloTest. Telomeres consist of repetitive DNA elements which protect the DNA string from degradation. They act as caps at the end of a DNA strand, a bit like the cap at the end of a shoelace. If that cap deteriorates, the shoe lace will unravel and it will be more difficult to thread it through a shoe. The same is true of telomeres. When they shorten and start to fray, they can no longer protect the DNA, signalling the end of the cell. Cell division is fundamental for the growth, development and repair of all living organisms, but repeated cell division results in dwindling telomeres. Every time a cell divides, and the chromosomes are copied, it loses a few bits at the end, resulting in telomere shortening. Cells can only divide a finite number of times, and when a cell reaches this limit, it either enters apoptosis ('commits suicide') or goes into senescence. Senescent cells are distressed cells that become senile. They undergo alterations and then signal their distress while clogging up valuable space meant for new cells. It is senescent cells that are responsible for inflammation and that contribute to ageing, among other processes.

Telomere dynamics in humans are affected by various environmental factors and complex pathways throughout our lifespans. Several studies show that psychological stress such as depression, anxiety and traumatic exposure accelerate telomere shortening.[6] Acute stress and injury lead to oxidative damage, which is when the body's cells produce free radicals during normal metabolic processes. The need for more energy impacts on cells, which in turn impacts on telomere lengths. Shortened telomeres accelerate ageing and inflammation, which is the root cause of chronic disease such as cancer, diabetes, heart and lung disease, cognitive decline and reduced immune function. They also explain why someone who has had psychological or physical trauma, prolonged sickness or surgery looks tired and haggard and experiences hair loss or whitening of the hair, reduced immunity, brain fog and failure to thrive. They become life-tired.

Other causes of telomere shortening are ultraviolet (UV) rays in sunlight, radiation from X-rays, chemicals, food and smoke. Recent developments in DNA testing can measure telomeres and give accurate predictions of the ageing of cells.

Senescent cells

There are cells that keep an eye on telomeres that are particularly susceptible to DNA damage and will 'programme' cell death when they detect heavy damage. Most cells respond to this order to self-destruct, but some persist. These are the senescent cells. They stick around and are dysfunctional; essentially, they have become senile. They no longer divide but continue to send distress signals and use up valuable resources by acting like zombies and eating cells in their immediate environment, chewing up collagen and the material that holds our cells together.[7] A significant presence of senescent cells clogs up space within our tissues, much needed for stem cells. The lack of stem cells directly impacts on the maintenance of our healthy cells. The constant repair and maintenance of cells taps our cell reserves, which leads to stem cell exhaustion.

Senescent cells can also change their function from blood cells to bone cells, leaving calcium deposits in veins that cause hardening of the blood vessels, resulting eventually in strokes and heart attacks. Senescent cells also cause widespread inflammation, known as 'inflammaging' ('inflame-ageing') or arthritis of the joints – something that is automatically associated with aches and pains in ageing.

None of us can escape damage to our cell structures, but in some individuals, like Mr H, the damage is far more profound.

From the moment the crocodile pulled him into the river, Mr H's body started releasing adrenaline, which enabled him to put up the biggest fight of his life. Adrenaline provides the initial energy required for this, but it only lasts a short time. Then in step cytokines, which are released by the stress response to initiate the complex inflammatory response. Cytokines signal the immune system to increase the heart rate, which increases oxygen use, and the respiratory rate, which provides the much-needed energy to preserve life. We require these responses for short-term survival, but if the trauma persists or is severe, it can lead to severe body damage within two to seven days and the body's functions will become impaired. Mr H's body was now eating itself, and he had minimal reserves to get him back on track. If we didn't address his sustenance, his body would continue to scavenge from the cells in various areas in his body, which can only divide a finite number of times.

As the days merged into weeks, Mr H failed to thrive. He was no longer at death's door, but he was not improving either. His condition was stable, and his wound was now free from gas gangrene and could finally be closed. However, despite his progress, he was fading – a result of his body's response to trauma. When he had arrived, he'd looked robust and powerful, and had a twinkle in his eye despite his injuries. The man in front of me now looked small and frail, with dull, hopeless eyes. He seemed to age daily, with sudden grey hair and hair loss. His muscles were wasting, and his left leg, shoulders and arms looked flaccid and emaciated. His skin was flaking and his wound healing seemed to have reached a plateau. He looked weak and had little energy. He was listless, disinterested and depressed.

He still had nightmares, and his sleep was constantly interrupted by twitching as he continued to fight his now familiar assailant. He would wake in a fugue state and stare wildly at his stump, clutching it and screaming for help. It was as if the croc was still latched to his leg.

We were still on the bottom two tiers of Maslow's Hierarchy. Before we could start his rehabilitation, we had to address his physiological and psychological needs. We needed to prevent further damage to his cells by reducing his anxiety and replenishing his energy through improved nutrition and better rest so that his body could recover.

His brain was functioning only at the most basic rate to ensure that he remained alive. It had no reserves to enable higher cognitive functions such as reading, taking an interest in his surroundings or actively engaging – the top tier of Maslow's Hierarchy. We have all felt like this at some point in our lives, especially after recovering from illness. It is what happens to our bodies when we are ill or injured, physically or mentally. The impact on Mr H was that he could not heal because he did not have the energy his body needed. The bad news is the shorter the telomeres, the higher the risk of death. The good news is that it is possible to reverse cellular ageing and improve telomere attrition.

Summary

None of us can escape damage to our cell structures. The exposure of our bodies to the onslaught of multiple events affects us at a cellular level. It is a multifaceted process, resulting in a progressive functional decline in cells, tissues and organisms.

2

Preventing Injury
And Ageing

The previous chapter explained how trauma, injury and disease change our body from within. They affect our endocrine (hormonal), metabolic and immune functions in several ways. Adequate nutritional support is imperative for survival, wellbeing and immunity. One of the reasons we age is that our bodies lack the nutrition that maintains the body's reserves.

Amino acids – the crucial fuel for our body

Each of us is a natural organism and, if we are to survive, we need energy. Energy must constantly flow through our organs, tissues and cells to sustain life. Even the processes of digestion, absorption and distribution require energy, and the production of energy requires nutrients.

We obtain nutrients from our dietary intake. They are metabolised into fuel and other molecules, which power cellular processes for energy production. Our primary fuel is amino acids, which carry out various functions that are vital for the maintenance of our tissues and organs. Amino acids are produced from proteins that the digestive system has broken down. There are twenty amino acids, all of which are needed daily to maintain the equilibrium within our bodies. Humans can produce only half of them; the rest must be 'added' via nutritional or supplemental intake. Our bodies need a steady stream of amino acids to promote healing and sustain health.

If your body lacks the vital amino acid to perform a specific function, it will cannibalise existing structures to replenish its dwindling amino acid pool. Your body will steal from itself, taking amino acids from areas such as the outside cover of vessel walls, skin and hair and, in the process, cause ageing.

Muscle power

We need a combination of amino acids in a specific order to make proteins, which are the building blocks for muscle and tissue in our body. If amino acid is lacking, the body cannot complete a specific metabolic process, which results in a delay in repair. Amino acids are generated by tiny organelles known as mitochondria. Thousands of these are present in our muscles and are responsible for generating protein and glucose, which provides energy. The more abundant our mitochondria, the more energy we have. Conversely, sarcopenia can negatively affect health, lifespan and quality of life. This is why an injury or trauma literally drains our life force. Maintaining amino acid reserves can prolong lifespan.

Free radicals hasten the ageing process

Our bodies – more particularly, our cells – are exposed to external daily assaults from our environment, such as UV light, smoke and exhaust fumes, and to internal metabolic processes. The combined external and internal processes influence the chemical reaction within our cells through the exchange of electrons known as oxidation.

During oxidation, oxygen molecules are split into single atoms, leading to unpaired electrons. The atoms that have lost an electron are now unstable and are known as a free radical, or reactive oxygen species (ROS). Free radicals desperately seek another atom to bond with and whizz around our cells in an attempt to restore their electromagnetic balance. They do this by stealing electrons from other atoms, starting a chain reaction.

The whizzing about of unstable atoms is known as oxidative stress and causes damage if left unchecked. Free radicals modify the biochemical patterns of cells and have a particular fondness for DNA. They stick to and change the genetic material of DNA, which can cause damage, mutations, immunosuppression and diseases, including cancer.

From the point of view of the ageing process, free radicals can lead to cell death or pathological cell and tissue damage such as dysfunctional skin, abnormal production of age spots, destruction of collagen and elastic fibres, poor healing and weakened blood vessels. In short, free radicals cause ageing.

Fortunately, our bodies have an oxidative defence system that protects us from free radicals, but only to a certain extent; when the system reaches its toxic threshold, it becomes insufficient to protect us. Antioxidants can reduce toxic levels and reverse cell damage. Supplements rich in antioxidants, such as vitamin C, green tea, berries, cloves and pomegranates, contribute electrons to free radicals and stop them whizzing around, restoring equilibrium.

Restoring balance

Another reason we age is that the body's reserves are depleted. In Mr H's case, his diet was not adequate to compensate for the battering his body had taken and enable it to repair itself internally. His body was undergoing a lot of repairs and required a lot of energy, with the result that he also had large amounts of free radicals whizzing around. It had become imperative that we involve dieticians and pharmacists to significantly improve his diet and nutritional supplementation. We did this through a combination of nutritionally dense foods called nutraceuticals. (Nutraceuticals are also used as part of a strategy against ageing, as I will explain later.)

Nutraceuticals are naturally derived bioactive compounds found in foods, dietary supplements or herbal products that have health-promoting, disease-preventing or medicinal properties. In other words, nutraceuticals are a concentrated form of a bioactive substance initially derived from food, providing a higher dose of that substance than regular food to enhance health.

The difference between oral supplementation and intravenous therapy is that oral supplements can lose up to 90% of their bioavailability – the extent to which a substance is available for its intended biological destination. Taking a supplement orally means that it first has to bypass the gut barrier, whereas receiving it intravenously means that it enters the circulation directly, resulting in a much more efficient and active delivery method. Further recent advances in technology provide nutraceuticals in droplet form through the mucous membrane of the mouth. This results in product absorption into the bloodstream within sixty to ninety seconds, further improving the delivery method and availability to the body. It is also far less invasive than a drip.

In Mr H's case, we used nutraceuticals in intravenous drips. We held a multidisciplinary team meeting in which nutritionists, biochemists and pharmacists joined forces to provide Mr H with an intravenous nutraceutical plan that included vital amino acids, minerals and vitamins as well as increased protein, fat and glucose.

However, treating Mr H's physical needs was not enough. We also needed to address those recurring nightmares. If Mr H was going to recover physically, we needed to repair him mentally and spiritually. Mind, body and soul must be in balance for a person to become and remain well.

Self-actualisation

Reverting to Maslow's Hierarchy of Needs, Mr H was still on the two lowest levels; we were taking care of his physiological and safety needs but not meeting his emotional or social needs. He was still far from being in control and thriving – something we needed to rectify as soon as possible. He was experiencing an overwhelming sense of grief.

Not only had he lost a limb, he had also lost a lifestyle, a way of life, including his passion for running and fishing, and his position among his family, friends and colleagues. He had a wife and a young family, who were now living alone on a remote farm, unprotected in turbulent times. He was a farmer and the primary breadwinner, with crops and animals and a team of seasonal workers who needed direction, especially in the planting season. Being deprived of all this was further impacting his wellbeing and starting to drive him towards a deep depression.

He could not see past his pain management and wound care. His continued hospitalisation and daily dependence on us meant that he had no purpose. He had lost control of his life. We were all treating him like a victim – showing him endless empathy and sympathy but not enabling him to pick up the pieces of his life and put them back together in a meaningful way.

What he needed now was love, affection and respect from his family, but his family was equally affected by every visit. They hovered and cried big-eyed in the corridors, and the youngest son was terrified every time he saw his dad. He was inconsolable and started bedwetting. Everybody looked haunted and unwell. I realised that we were so busy with Mr H that we had neglected his family and their combined needs. It was then that I understood the crucial importance of taking a holistic approach to everybody's wellness. I arranged a family and friend counselling session to start a process for everyone involved.

After any traumatic event, it is not possible to move forwards unless we have absolute clarity about what happened to us. Up to this point, nobody who had witnessed Mr H's horrific accident had shared their memories of what had taken place on that fateful day. It was a cathartic moment for everyone involved, including me.

It turned out that the crocodile had attacked Mr H not once, but twice. When he was first attacked, Mr H vigorously battled the croc in front of his friends and children, who all fought to drag him from the croc's jaws and stem the bleeding. They rested Mr H on the side of the river bank, leaving him momentarily alone while they ran to get help and calm the traumatised children. As Mr H caught his breath, the croc returned and dragged him back towards the water, trying to tear away the partially severed leg. In the cacophony, a hippo came to Mr H's rescue. It ran towards the crocodile, chasing it back into the water. Witnessing this, Mr H's friends and family were stunned and certain that he would be injured further. The hippo was gentle, though, and took care not to hurt the wounded man. It followed the croc back into the river, making sure it was no longer a threat.

That day, elephants had been grazing quietly nearby, and they witnessed the whole event. As the hippo emerged from the water and sniffed to check Mr H, the elephants began to trumpet loudly. This startled the birds, and the forest came alive with the sounds of the animals, which all seemed to cheer along.

Mr H had lost consciousness from shock and exhaustion when the crocodile returned for its second attack, so hadn't known of these events until everyone sat down together in a room and shared their recollections. What he learned from this story, relayed to him by his family and six- and seven-year-old children, was that he was not meant to die. It was this realisation that brought about the most significant change in his condition. The story of his survival awoke a deep spiritual response within Mr H, and he immediately became resolute. Knowing that his social circle of family and friends needed him to get better, he moved into the next tier of Maslow's Hierarchy. He had been given a purpose: to get home and get on with his life.

Soon, Mr H was ready to return to his family and begin his new life, leaving me and our team changed.

Summary

Each of us is a natural organism and, if we are to survive, we need energy. The production of energy requires nutrients. One of the reasons we age is that our bodies lack the nutrition that maintains the body's reserves.

3

The Keys To Wellness

My profound experience with Mr H and his family set me on my current course. Thirty-one years later, I am still learning from it. Mr H taught me the importance of considering mind, body and soul in every patient contact – the need to truly listen and see deeply. Mr H's journey continued, and his resolution that he was not meant to die that day drove him to make a full recovery with the help of a prosthetic limb. The takeaway is that there is always hope, and that hope impacts us on a deep, cellular level.

I have used Mr H's story to show that what happened to Mr H's body is also happening to ours. The crocodile that attacked him is symbolic of all the negative things that happen to us. We are all fighting crocodiles throughout our lives, and the impact of that struggle on our mind, body and soul is the same as on Mr H's. The damage that is done to our bodies may be more insidious – a gradual process rather than a sudden shocking event – but the effects are essentially the same:

- Anxiety and stress impact on our cortisol, which reduces the effectiveness of hormones such as progesterone (the feel-good hormone).

- A stress response leads to reduced immunity and greater susceptibility to disease.

- Stress creates accelerated hypermetabolism, increasing our body's demand for energy, but we already feel energy-depleted due to our habits and lifestyle.

- A large proportion of us don't have great diets, which means that our body is having to adapt by scavenging from itself, leaving us susceptible to further injury and disease.

- We associate dieting with weight loss or prevention of chronic disease and don't appreciate that our diet can be used to age less.

- Fad diets that prevent us from getting the right nourishment and balance can actually be harmful and lead to chronic disease or reduced immunity.

- Muscles are energy stores and the more muscle we have, the more energy we have – hence the advice to exercise to build muscle.

- Sarcopenia correlates with shortened life span.

All of the above impact our telomeres, shortening our health span. Shortened telomeres lead to a shorter life.

For these reasons, too many of us fail to thrive, and it is time we did things differently.

Daily damage

Our lives are not one single easy road. They follow a meandering path strewn with events and experiences that expose us to the elements, injuries and illnesses which impact our health and wellbeing. We suffer daily stress and anxiety caused by work, family, relationships, money, world news and so on. We are victim to various assaults, from a simple cold or a broken bone to a significant event such as a serious illness, a stroke or heart attack. Each time, our bodies take a hit. We see it in our eyes, hair and skin; we feel it in our muscles, joints and bones. A cold lingers, a wound takes longer than it should to heal, we have post-viral fatigue. We suffer hair, bone and muscle loss; we feel miserable and depressed. Our wellbeing is compromised.

Wellness models

Wellbeing means a balanced physical, social, emotional, spiritual and financial life. Wellness is the optimal state of wellbeing, where a person is not only balanced in all dimensions but also vital, thriving and in control; where they are in a position to choose the attitudes and lifestyle they want to adopt and can take care of themselves.

For me, the three crucial dimensions of wellness are the physical, the social and the emotional. Think of a waiter carrying a tray with one hand above his head on which three full glasses of water are equally balanced. If you were to remove one glass, the whole tray would suddenly become unbalanced and crash to the floor. Our bodies are like this tray: they become unwell when one of the elements is missing, which sets them off balance, creating a knock-on effect that spirals out of control.

There are several other, more sophisticated, wellness models and the science is constantly evolving, with new dimensions being added all the time. The best-known wellness model incorporates not three but six elements: physical, social, emotional, mental, spiritual and environmental. If any one of these elements is missing or deficient, homeostasis is lost.

The wellness economy

The wellness economy is thriving at $4.5 trillion[8] – more than half of total global health expenditure (see the table below) – and, according to the Global Wellness Institute,[9] predicted to continue growing. People are now better informed and able to choose alternative therapies and personalised care, avoiding medication. The fastest-growing trends are in aesthetics, skincare, personalised nutrition, menopause treatments and hair growth. The most significant growth areas are in the nutritional market, estimated to be worth over $123 billion in 2019 and growing at 8.2%. The menopause market is expected to be worth over $6 billion by 2027.[10]

Wellness economy spending

Sector	Expenditure value
Total global health expenditure	£7.8 trillion
Wellness economy total	$4.5 trillion
Preventative and personalised medicine	$575 billion
Beauty and anti-ageing	$1.083 trillion
Nutrition and weight loss	$702 billion
Mind and body	$639 billion

A holistic approach

Before setting up my clinic, I worked in a GP practice on a large university campus. I was struck by how unwell young people are. They are exhausted, their sleep is interrupted, they succumb to stress, anxiety and all sorts of minor illnesses. When they are stressed (emotional health), they cannot eat or sleep (physical health) and they become withdrawn (social health). Their moods are so low that they struggle even to get out of bed. Adults do not fare much better. Common symptoms include bowel disease, stress, anxiety, menopausal symptoms and failure to thrive.

The differences between the younger and older generation are financial income, independence and poor lifestyle choices. The younger generation skip meals, but also live more unhealthily now that they have to cook for themselves. They lean towards fast foods and binge drinking and are more exposed to disease, hence the phenomenon of 'freshers' flu', a name commonly given to a battery of illnesses contracted by new students during their first weeks at university. I started to investigate their blood and found that most of their parameters were at the low end of normal or completely depleted, especially their bone profiles and levels of vitamin B12 and vitamin D, iron, zinc and folate (vitamin B9).

Even greater impact is due to their social world, which is disrupted by moving away from home and family and, in many cases, exposure to a new culture and language. Some students experience bereavement because they have moved abroad, left family and loved ones and are not able to adapt and meet the increased demands of university life without their familiar support network. These changes disrupt their physical, social and emotional worlds and their suffering is exacerbated by social media. They feel they don't fit in, or are not as cool, they don't have the same number of followers or people don't like their posts, etc. It is no wonder that so many students crash and burn. For many students, we offer counselling (which has long waiting lists), but they often reattend with worsening symptoms, or seek other 'solutions' such as antidepressants.

Out with the old, in with the new

The NHS landscape is incredibly complex, and the majority of the workload is focused on managing chronic disease. We are living longer thanks to technology, but this means that there are 'almost 12 million people aged sixty-five and over in the UK, with 3.2 million aged eighty and over. It's estimated that by 2036, one in four of the population will be over sixty-five.'[11] While health conditions are not inevitable with age, the likelihood of having one or more long-term conditions, such as musculoskeletal problems, circulatory problems and Type 2 diabetes, does increase. GP practices are given incentives to manage chronic disease, which exacerbates the focus on managing and treating symptoms, rather than spending time and resources on prevention or seeking the causes of ageing.

Service delivery is determined by clinical commissioning groups (CCGs), which are groups of general practices working together in each area to commission the best services for their patients and population. The CCGs determine what money to spend where and on what services. As a result, there is a disparity between services, depending on the population groups and number of practices within the CCGs. Working in various GP practices across several counties, I have had to adapt to different prescribing practices, and budget restrictions mean that I have to prescribe the cheapest products despite the multitude of side effects. The situation is compounded by the prohibition of certain treatments – for example, joint injections for arthritis or prescribing for menopause. This practice is for cost reasons and results in the deskilling of doctors and other medical practitioners.

I have also had to reduce the amount of blood tests and access to services to keep referral rates to specialists down – again for cost-saving reasons. Not all practices have enough GPs with specialist knowledge. For example, some practices have gynaecological endocrinology and paediatric experts and others not. Some have surgeons and orthopaedic specialists, others not. The result is unequal access to services and service delivery built around a one-size-fits-all philosophy.

Practices are overloaded, with daily caseloads of around forty patients, each of whom must be seen in a ten-minute period. This includes introductions, taking a history, examining the body, diagnosing the problem and developing a treatment plan. In between those slots, GPs must handle phone calls from patients, staff members and laboratories, as well as admin tasks such as filing bloods and writing sick notes or referral letters to colleagues. It is no wonder that doctors are burning out and reducing their hours, further impacting on the case load.

There are new advances all the time, and these are picked up by the media and widely publicised, but always with the message to 'see your GP'. It is great to raise awareness, but this further impacts the already overloaded health service. There are only so many hours in the day, which means that it is hard to find the time to look at alternative treatments, run clinical trials or think outside the box when exhausted and overworked.

Patients further increase the caseload by expecting everything 'instantly' and for free. Today's society expects a twenty-four-hour service and a rapid response. We are used to receiving a service at the click of a button and expect the same when it comes to our health. Patients want quick fixes, and many prefer a tablet over a watch-and-wait approach or taking some responsibility, which places the responsibility and burden of their health on someone else. There are multiple reasons for this, such as lack of support networks and education, and not understanding their bodies and the impact that their lifestyle has on their body and wellbeing.

The result is that medicine is no longer fit for purpose and needs to change. Change cannot be left with healthcare providers and healthcare systems; it has to become everybody's business. Placing the entire burden on the NHS and relying solely on 'reactive' treatment is not sustainable. Preventive and personalised health with early intervention and management is the way forward.

We need to have a paradigm shift in the way we approach our own health. Patients will pay large amounts for plastic surgery or noninvasive cosmetics and aesthetics, cosmetics, hairdressing, gym membership, supplements and holidays but they are loath to invest in their own health. Cellular ageing can be slowed down with the right approach, minimising and even reducing chronic disease and resulting in better ageing or even agelessness. The challenge is one of education and functional medicine. What can we do ourselves to prevent our bodies from ageing?

Summary

Everybody has the right to live a well-balanced life. Experience, technology and innovation make it possible for us all to receive personalised care, enabling us to live optimised in every way. In this book I aim to pave the way towards that goal by raising awareness of how life impacts and ages us, and of the measures that can help minimise those impacts. When we understand our bodies better, we are equipped with more knowledge on how to rectify most problems and with that information can change our lives and support ourselves towards ageing less.

Medicine is limited to fixing the inside of our bodies when things have gone wrong, while the aesthetic industry is so focused on treating the outside with fillers, Botox and skincare products that it completely misses – or intentionally ignores – what is happening under the skin to cause the visible signs of ageing. There is a whole other side that can reduce ageing at a cellular level and support patients emotionally and physically. It can give patients a better quality of life and wellbeing and possibly enhance aesthetic treatment even further. Ageing requires both an inside and an outside approach, bringing the art of functional medicine (reversing ageing) together with aesthetics (looking better), to support an individual in living healthier for longer.

Part Two

GETTING UNDER THE SKIN

It is time to reset our thinking and raise awareness about the hidden regenerative opportunities inside our bodies which contribute to us dying unnecessarily young or living a less optimised life. Using ageing as an excuse is no longer acceptable. We can live better for longer without inflammation and chronic disease and have a better quality of life.

The key to this revolution is changing the perception that nutrition is solely associated with dieting or chronic disease and using nutrition to prevent injury or illness. The aim of nutrition now is to prevent ageing, not disease. There is now a move away from recommended daily allowances (RDAs), which assume that a population are healthy, rather than considering when someone isn't healthy. We have learned that we need adequate muscle and nutrition to live and feel well. Without sufficient nutrition, our bodies will scavenge it elsewhere within them, depleting our DNA pool and causing us to age. The question is: How do we know the nutritional needs of our bodies without guessing?

In the following chapters, I delve into new DNA technologies and supplementation through tablets and intravenous drips and explain their role in achieving agelessness. I also address the question of biohacking and examine phenomena such as hair loss and the menopause, including andropause in men, providing you with ways of reducing the ageing impact of depleted hormones.

4

Hair Loss

Hair is one of the most striking and defining aspects of a person's appearance. Throughout history, hair has mirrored the cultural zeitgeist. An example is the ancient Greeks and Romans. The more intricate their hairstyle, the higher their status. In the thirteenth and fourteenth centuries, long braided hair was a person's 'crowning glory'. Apart from fashion trends, hairstyles convey political messages and are a visible expression of what is happening in society. Consider the outrageous wigs worn by Marie Antoinette or the Mohawk of 1970s punks. Flowing locks have always represented sexiness and confidence. Hair also represents a particular lifestyle, an outlook that defines a person. You can tell a lot about someone by the way they wear their hair.

Alopecia, or losing hair, can be devastating. It means a loss of identity and, for many, their sense of self. It can cause all genders extreme stress and anxiety, and, of course, it is one of the most common and noticeable effects of ageing.

Causes of hair loss

The most common causes of alopecia are:

- Hormonal changes

- Stress and anxiety

- Vitamin and mineral deficiencies

- Endocrine disease

- Autoimmune deficiencies

- Effects of hair styling / heat

- Medication

- Reduced blood flow to the hair follicles

Alopecia is a progressive condition with different causes and there are equally different types. The most common are androgenic alopecia, areata alopecia and telogen effluvium (TE).

Androgenic alopecia, also known as male or female pattern baldness, is usually inherited and is caused by an androgen hormone such as testosterone and dihydrotestosterone. The cause is hormone dysregulation. Alopecia areata is related to autoimmune dysfunction, but the hair follicles remain preserved. It usually presents in small bald patches but can progress to total loss. TE is the increased shedding of normal hair caused mainly by triggers such as trauma, illness, medication and nutrition. I suffered from TE.

Hair loss treatments are a multibillion-dollar industry, and the market is flooded with hair regeneration and hair replacement products to the extent that we can easily be overwhelmed and not know where to start.

My hair loss journey

Around my early forties, I experienced severe hair loss. My hair went from a thick mane to the thin trickle of a ponytail. I could feel the cold wind on my scalp – something previously utterly alien to me – and my hair looked awful. It was thin and broken, and I was shedding it everywhere; it came out in clumps every time I washed it. They say that stress causes hair loss, but how do you avoid being stressed when your crown is slipping away at such an alarming rate? I was becoming anxious, emotional and desperate. I cut my hair short and started researching. I threw everything I could at my recovery.

I appreciated for the first time how my hundreds of patients felt, how genuinely devastating hair loss was for them. From my own experience I knew that there was not much anybody could do, apart from a few blood tests to exclude the obvious hormonal problem. When levels of oestrogen and progesterone drop, hair grows more slowly and becomes thinner. A decrease in these hormones also triggers an increase in the production of androgens, a group of male hormones. Androgens shrink hair follicles, resulting in hair loss. Lack of iron or vitamin D are other hair loss culprits. At the time, the only two treatments for hair loss on the market were finasteride and minoxidil, both of which patients could buy over the counter. Dermatologists might prescribe a steroid cream if the cause was inflammation. Although there were successes, in the majority of cases patients had poor outcomes or, worse, awful side effects.

What frustrated me most was the fatalistic approach adopted by medical professionals: that I must simply accept my lot because I was 'of a certain age'. No way was I going to admit defeat and 'live with it', gracefully or otherwise. There had to be another way, but little did I know how long it would take and how many different treatment modalities I would have to try before I finally achieved success.

The first treatment I tried was carboxytherapy.

Carboxytherapy

Carboxytherapy is based on a 1904 discovery that carbon dioxide reacts with water to produce carbonic acid.[12] Strangely, this reduces the acidity of body tissues, which in turn prompts them to release oxygen. The increased oxygen means an increased flow of nutrients to that area. It also dilates the capillaries (blood vessels), increases the blood flow and stimulates an inflammatory, or healing, response that boosts collagen, improving the skin's structure. The skin texture and tone improve because of the reorganisation of collagen.

Collagen is a protein that is abundant in our bodies. It is made up of amino acids and provides structural support to our hair, skin, bones, tendons and ligaments. Wounding the skin results in collagen formation. Twenty-eight types of collagen have been discovered. Collagen VI is abundant in the skin and hair follicles.

Carboxytherapy is the delivery of carbon dioxide gas into the body using a tiny needle tip. It is a popular therapy because it is 'natural' and has minimal side effects. Carbon dioxide is a naturally occurring gas essential for breathing and vital for survival. We expel it through our lungs as a by-product of breathing.

Carboxytherapy destroys fat cells and widens smooth muscle, which normally contracts but is now relaxed, resulting in increased oxygen flow to that area and a reduction in pain, especially in wounds. The gas flows into the tissues under specific pressures, causing 'injury' to the tissues, which stimulates fibroblasts. Fibroblasts are responsible for signalling numerous growth factors responsible for the production of collagen and connective tissue.

Carboxytherapy originated in French spas in the 1930s and today it is used to treat a variety of conditions, including cellulite, stretch marks, scars and dark under-eye circles; it is also used for fat reduction, leg ulcers, leg oedema (swollen legs due to fluid), vaginal dryness and complicated wounds. The following case studies illustrate the diverse uses and effectiveness of carboxytherapy.

Case study: Facial carboxytherapy

A female patient of mine received a devastating facial injury. The wounds to her face were painful and there was a considerable risk of scarring. When wounds heal, collagen is produced, but because of the damage the collagen becomes disrupted, which results in tethering or puckering of the skin. In this case, the uneven collagen deposits pulled the patient's mouth down in the corner and bulged around her chin.

She received six sessions of carboxytherapy, which immediately resulted in shrinking of the wound and releasing of the tethering. Within three months, the scar had faded to a faint silver line with no deformity to her face. She continued to make a full recovery.

Case study: Cat bite

One day, I attempted to rescue a distressed cat that was in danger of being run over. Unfortunately, the incident did not end well – for me, not the cat. In its fear, the cat clawed and bit my fingers on both hands. The outcome was a visit to A&E, followed by a referral to hand surgeons for dressings, antibiotics and an imminent theatre slot to wash out the wounds. I was soon discharged but a follow-up appointment revealed that my wounds might worsen as a result of infection from the cat bite.

All the fingers were swollen, discoloured and incredibly painful. Injecting carbon dioxide directly into the open wounds resulted in vasodilation of the surrounding tissues, which immediately relieved my pain, making it more bearable, and resulted in quicker healing.

Carboxytherapy for hair loss

Both the needle pricks and the gas flowing into the tissue cause the body to recognise that the tissue has been breached and to signal fibroblasts to start healing. Fibroblasts in turn signal collagen to close the wound. The gas creates an acid, which the body needs to get rid of by flooding the area with oxygen, bringing further growth factors. The combined growth factors from fibroblasts and oxygen rapidly increase healing. Since the wounding of skin results in collagen formation, carboxytherapy is ideal for hair loss. The injury to the scalp also prompts angiogenesis, or the formation of new blood vessels, and the carbon dioxide gas stimulates the body to flood the area with oxygen. The result is collagen formation around the hair bulb and follicles.

Despite the many benefits of carboxytherapy, the results in my case were slow and mediocre. In some patients the treatment works well and in others it doesn't. The reason for this is still unknown. What was heartening was that I could see a lot of new fuzz, which meant that there was new hair growth. However, I was still shedding large amounts of hair. My quest for a hair loss solution continued.

I tried growth factors, the vampire method and nutraceuticals – techniques that are also used to treat fine lines, stretch marks, scars and other skin problems – all with limited success. It was not until DNA testing became available that I found the solution that worked for me, thanks to the DNA TrichoTest.

DNA TrichoTest

The DNA TrichoTest, which was developed by the Belgian company Fagron Genomics, uses genetics to determine the causes of hair loss and isolate the best treatment for each individual case.

Genetic testing allows a comprehensive genomic characterisation of a specific condition in a specific individual to be obtained. It enables the causes of diseases unique to that person to be determined and treatment tailored accordingly and accurately. It can improve outcomes as well as save money on costly treatments. Baldness is now indeed a choice.

The aims of the TrichoTest are:

- Prediction and prevention

- More precise diagnosis

- Targeted personalised interventions

- A more participatory role for the patient

The test is obtained the same way as the nutrigenomic and TeloTest, by taking a salivary sample from the inside of your mouth which is then sent off for DNA analysis by a geneticist and immunologist. In combination with a pharmacist, they recommend a treatment regime. It costs £250 and is available in the UK from various clinics.

The TrichoTest analyses forty-eight genetic variations on the most relevant mutations related to alopecia, as well as several lifestyle factors, and suggests personalised treatment accordingly.

The factors that are tested for include:

- Hormonal changes

- Vitamin and mineral deficiencies

- Endocrine disease

- Autoimmune disease

- Effects of hair styling / heat

- Effects of the use of medication

My results – a twelve-page analysis of all of the above – revealed the causes of my hair loss: my circulation was compromised and I had reduced blood flow to my scalp. The report recommended that I increase my intake of caffeine or apply it directly to my scalp. I also had a problem with collagen synthesis to my scalp, and a product called cysteine was recommended. Cysteine is a nonessential amino acid normally produced within the body, but not in my case.

Investigating cysteine, I discovered a whole lot more about my ageing process than I had expected. To make cysteine, I needed adequate folate, vitamins B12 and B6, which I did not have – as shown by my nutrigenomic test. You will remember that when one link in the vital chain of vitamins, minerals and amino acids is missing, it has an impact all along the chain. Because I did not have adequate amounts of vitamin B6, I could not make cysteine, and because I could not make cysteine, I was now suffering hair loss. We can obtain cysteine from high-protein foods such as turkey, chicken, yogurt, cheese, eggs, sunflower seeds and legumes, so I needed to increase my intake of those.

I further discovered that cysteine is required for many biological functions in the body and reduces cell death. It is necessary to make taurine (an ingredient in Red Bull), which is essential for our nervous system and brain development. Cysteine is a potent antioxidant and pacifies free radicals, which can cause DNA damage and cancer. Cysteine also helps with dopamine function and disease symptoms such as tremors; it helps chronic breathing conditions, improves fertility and helps prevent liver and kidney damage. It detoxes the body and prevents damage from environmental toxins. It improves the symptoms of bipolar disease and depression. Lastly, but importantly, it plays a part in hair and skincare.

The value of this second genetic test was equally huge. I could now supplement my diet with products recommended for hair loss. It is essential to note that what is suitable for one person isn't necessarily good for another. My test report informed me that I did not need Biotin (vitamin B7), but suggested that I supplement with Q10, a coenzyme that is important in the mitochondria (remember, these are the energy providers in the muscle). Q10 improves heart function, but it also helps lower blood pressure. I did not have high blood pressure, but I had an angiotensin-converting enzyme 2 (ACE2) problem, which affected the blood circulation to my scalp. ACE2s narrow blood vessels, which can cause high blood pressure and force the heart to work harder but, in the scalp, it reduces blood flow to the hair follicle. Taking a Q10 supplement, I managed to increase the blood flow to my scalp.

Did all this help? Many roads ultimately lead to the top of the mountain. Some are quicker and others more arduous. Along any journey in life new opportunities arise alongside new insights and discoveries. Through DNA testing for hair loss, I ultimately achieved a solution and am thankful to have my thick, lustrous mane back and to be feeling my old self again.

Summary

There are many new technologies with potentially unmeasurable benefits which will ultimately change medicine and wellbeing as we understand it. Addressing and treating the causes of hair loss is just one area in which this can be seen.

5

Nutrition And Nutraceuticals

When people hear the word nutrition, they usually associate it with diet and losing weight, rarely with ageing. For years, women – especially those aged around forty-five to fifty – have been told that 'ideal' beauty is associated with a more petite body. The aim is to be smaller, which means dieting and eating less. Some become self-conscious about what they eat, to the point of self-imposed starvation, forgetting that a grown woman's body is not thin and flat, with lean muscle, but curved, with wide hips and adipose tissue. In fact, when you look at the history of diet culture, weight gain is associated with normal ageing, creating a contradiction. Our bodies will gain weight due to ageing, but we want to remain youthful, and to achieve that, we try to become slimmer.

It is no wonder that when we hear the word nutrition we think of dieting, calorie counting, food weighing, weight loss, guilt and body shaming, being constantly reminded of our 'unhealthy' lifestyle and the need for change, especially now that we are getting older. We might take supplements to prevent certain diseases or for diagnosed health problems, but we seldom think that supplements can go further, preventing ageing of our cells, which leads to chronic disease and a less optimised life.

The truth about nutrition

In fact, nutrition is about far more than managing our weight. Bodily changes are due largely to nutrition. People of all ages need more than forty nutrients to stay healthy. The consumption of critical reserves for body maintenance and continuation of normal function are the two main reasons for compromised health and wellness, which in turn curtails longevity. Our diet alone is inadequate for providing nutrition for optimal health and requires optimisation through oral or intravenous supplementation – potentially in quite large quantities. Recommended dietary vitamin intakes do not begin to reflect the levels required for optimal health.[13]

Routine blood tests are used to analyse various components within our body and how well our organs are working. They help us to diagnose disease, injury, infection and inflammation and specify 'normal' levels of nutritional components such as vitamins and minerals. 'Normal' ranges can be extremely wide: for vitamin D, for example, 'normal' levels are between 50 and 150 ng/ml, and for vitamin B12 between 190 and 950 pg/ml. Endocrinology specialists suggest that essential nutrients should be kept at between 75% and 100% of the upper end of those ranges,[14] and argue that many people need one or more vitamins and antioxidants far in excess of recommended levels for optimal health.[15]

Measuring the levels of vitamins B6 and B12 and folic acid, for example, provides inadequate information. Measuring homocysteine levels is a much better indicator of the right amounts of vitamins B6, B12 and folic acid. High levels of homocysteine indicate inflammation within the body and point to a higher risk of cardiovascular disease, Alzheimer's and mood disorders. What is adequate for one person is not necessarily adequate for another.[16] The aim in nutrition should be to optimise and improve general wellbeing and not only to prevent deficiency diseases or address specific conditions.[17] Among other potential benefits, supplements can prevent memory loss, support the immune system, help hair regrowth, improve muscles and energy, and reduce the effect of menopause or premenstrual problems.

There are many causes of nutritional deficiencies. Poor agricultural soil caused by intensive farming, which depletes the fertility and nutritional value of the land; the way food is stored and cooked; poor dietary habits and poverty all affect the amount and variety of nutrient-rich foods available to the individual. Disease, medication and poor absorption due to gut problems can impair the uptake of vitamins and minerals within the body. As people age, cells within their intestinal tract become less active and therefore less adequate to digest and absorb nutrients, especially vitamin B12. The lack of even one nutrient can lead to various diseases and DNA damage. For instance, lack of iron can cause breathlessness, light-headedness, fatigue and straining of the heart. Lack of vitamin D can cause reduced immunity, painful joints and bone-related problems, hair loss, headaches and low moods. Lack of vitamin B12 increases cysteine levels, leading to inflammation.

Remember Mr H, whose cells started to scavenge from his reserves to heal his wounds and let him survive? It left him a thin, skeletal mess with thinning hair. Our bodies need vitamins, minerals and amino acids assembled in specific combinations for us to survive, let alone thrive. When there is a lack of any of the nutritional elements the body cannot complete the process, known as a metabolic pathway. The effect is that it delays repair, reduces energy production or allows free radicals to accumulate, which leads to DNA damage and potentially cancer or various other diseases. As discussed in previous chapters, the body will always try to complete the pathway but, if it lacks nutritional elements, it will scavenge from itself. The result is bodily changes which further compromise health and wellness and ultimately curtail longevity. The functional decline of our cells is what causes us to age. If we can avoid our body borrowing from itself, we will prevent our cells from declining and minimise the impact of ageing.

My experience with Mr H and other patients led me to realise that there was another way of looking at nutrition – not just as a mechanism to lose weight. Further research revealed a method that is specific and personalised to the individual, refuting the one-size-fits-all philosophy of so many diet 'plans'. A way that tells you what your body's specific food requirements are for wellbeing, and that can predict your risk of chronic disease, allowing you time to make the changes before it is too late. A way that provides you with an accurate summary of what to avoid and what to eat, specific to your body, and tells you exactly what you require and what vitamins your body doesn't make, what your body doesn't tolerate. A way to avoid endless food diaries, trial and error and guesswork.

Thanks to modern science, nutrition is available in various formats such as infusions, injections and nanotechnology, where it is administered through the mucosa in the mouth, preventing issues caused by mal-absorption in the gut. The exciting difference between pharmaceutical drugs and nutrition is that drugs aim to treat one problem with one drug. Nutrition, on the other hand, provides a multitude of chemical molecules which regulate different biological processes. Don't forget that food is a drug too, so one drug can treat a variety of problems. During my hair loss quest, I came across a company called IntraVita which manufactures nutraceuticals – intravenous nutrition that claims to 'uplift, energise, rejuvenate and enhance performance and wellbeing'.[18] Nutraceuticals do not make claims to cure disease but support the body to function optimally. This was the start of my journey into nutraceuticals.

Nutraceuticals

I learned more about nutraceuticals from Dr Jacques Otto. He is not only a doctor who specialises in various fields, including medical pharmacology, sedation and pain control, but also an outstanding athlete who com-peted in the Olympics. His knowledge and experience in medical pharmacology and as an athlete helped him realise the impact of exercise on the body and the need for adequate nutrition and recovery. He works closely with various organisations in the EU and Asia to develop intravenous nutritional treatment plans for wellness.

Having spoken to Dr Otto, I decided to research and critically analyse nutraceuticals for my dissertation in aesthetic medicine.[19] I had a profound personal reason to find a cure and solution for hair loss, wellbeing and agelessness, and I wanted to make a difference in my patients' lives.

'Nutraceuticals' is another hybrid word, derived from 'nutrition' and 'pharmaceuticals', to describe supplements that provide a specific health benefit. Nutraceuticals combine vitamins, minerals, amino acids and plant-based preparations. They are dietary supplements that exceed the amounts of these substances in everyday food. Dietary intervention can positively reduce ageing and prevent or decrease age-related diseases and proinflammatory status provided that critical amino acid reserves are maintained. As we have seen, our bodies can only produce ten of the twenty amino acids they need; our food intake must supply the rest. This requires an integrated approach to nutraceuticals and functional foods as a strategy against ageing – to enable us to move beyond the baseline requirements for survival and enjoy a higher quality of life.

Nutraceuticals comprise a cocktail of vitamins, minerals and amino acids mixed into a drip and administered intravenously – a treatment known as an infusion. Infusions allow greater bioavailability because the substances enter the circulation and have an active and more immediate effect. Infusions are widely used in Asia, parts of Europe (especially Germany) and America, where it has become a new fad for company directors to have intravenous drips during meetings to improve brain power and performance. Despite their popularity abroad, they do not seem to have taken off in the UK, where we tend to rely on the good old NHS – largely, perhaps, because it is free. It seems strange that we are happy to pay for holidays, entertainment and aesthetic treatments, but we leave it to the NHS to sort out our health, which is more important than any of those things.

Nutraceutical treatment options

Nutraceuticals can be administered as a capsule or via infusions and are available in concentrated form in single or combination substances. I prefer combination infusions because various nutrients perform different tasks based on your specific needs, including:

- Energy boosting

- Detoxing

- Skin brightening

- Hair and nail nourishment

- Heavy metal removal

- Muscle recovery after training

- Boosting athletic performance

- Boosting metabolism

To obtain my master's degree I not only had to sit a great many exams, but was also required to work full time in a busy GP practice. Much of the time I felt exhausted and struggled to concentrate. I started to infuse myself before exams and during dissertations, and I also did so when writing this book. This gave me better brain clarity and concentration levels and a sense of improved wellbeing.

The first time I had an infusion was like nothing else I had ever experienced. It was only then that I realised that I had not been functioning optimally. My brain fog and tiredness cleared. The following week, I experienced an increased energy boost that helped me immensely with my studies and exams. My skin looked great, and I had a new vitality. I did not realise that I had been feeling anxious until I woke up and discovered that nothing bothered me: not delayed trains, not the rush to work, not my workload of over forty patients a day at ten-minute intervals. I felt well, calm, clear and ready to tackle anything.

I had two colleagues at the clinic, and both were struggling with concerns. One suffered from fibromyalgia and low energy. The other experienced frequent styes in her eye and was not thriving. I treated them both with a double shot of glutathione, which is a superantioxidant. Both women felt better within hours, and those styes cleared up and have not returned to this day.

The following case study illustrates the effect nutraceuticals can have.

Case study: Angie

I truly appreciated nutraceuticals in the case of Angie. Angie was fifty-seven years old when her husband of twenty-five years died suddenly and unexpectedly one evening. She found him fighting for breath in their garden and administered CPR, but was unable to save him. She had three children, her eldest about to start university. Angie was an athlete and ran several miles a day, as well as doing other exercise, for her wellbeing. She was naturally anxious and worked all hours. The results were visible: lax, dull skin; wasted muscles; limp, thinning hair; brittle nails; and a look of defeat and pain.

Even before her husband's death, she had not been thriving but was constantly tired and forgetful, and outwardly appeared worn out. The loss of her husband had made things worse. She stopped running and exercising, which reduced her production of the feel-good hormones serotonin and dopamine. Serotonin is responsible for stabilising mood, feelings of wellbeing and happiness, while dopamine is the brain's reward system. It is no wonder that Angie was on her knees. She wouldn't eat for days, and her body responded by further depleting her hair and skin, which also broke out in cold sores on her nose and mouth and large patches of eczema. She did not sleep well and kept waking up in a dream state or crying throughout the night.

When Angie walked through my door, I was shocked. She looked both ill and miserable. She had come to me because she wanted to make herself feel better and thought some Botox and fillers would do the trick. I convinced Angie to instead go down a nourishment route and invest in nutraceuticals. I started her on a drip, and within minutes she was asleep. As she slept, I took her blood pressure and pulse every fifteen minutes, and it was fascinating to see how her body changed. Her skin colour changed from pale to pink, and her dry lips became soft and moisturised. She slept deeply, and I let her for a couple of hours. When she awoke, she hopped off the bed and hugged me, saying that she hadn't felt so well in ages.

I treated Angie a few more times. Her cold sores and eczema cleared up. Because she was sleeping well, she could deal mentally with everything better, and her body was healing physically. She was starting to get out running again and had restored her equilibrium socially.

Correct supplementation

The supplement market is expanding exponentially and was valued at $140.3 billion in 2020.[20] Supplements for health and wellness followed by immunity are consumers' most significant priorities when it comes to their health. Supplements can become an expensive commodity when we consider the amounts we can take each day over many years, so it's important to choose the right ones. How do we decide which supplements to buy?

Most producers offer a vitamin complex that has 'everything' needed by adults or children but, as we have seen, needs are individual and cannot be 'averaged out' in a generic way. Most people are not tested for their supplement needs unless they are unwell and have seen their doctors. Even then, the tests performed are usually limited and cover only a few basics such as vitamin B12, folate and iron. Most of the time we buy supplements blindly, unaware that we need to combine certain supplements to ensure better absorption and that our bodies will not use some unless another is also taken, as in the example of vitamin D and calcium. Vitamin D should always be taken along with calcium because the body needs vitamin D to absorb calcium.

Summary

Nutrition is about far more than managing our weight. Bodily changes are due largely to nutrition. Our bodies need vitamins, minerals and amino acids assembled in specific combinations for us to survive, let alone thrive. When there is a lack of any of the nutritional elements the body cannot complete the process, resulting in delayed repair, reduced energy production or the accumulation of free radicals, leading to DNA damage and potentially cancer or other diseases.

6

Using Nutritional Technology To Age Less

I am now in my fifties and over the years have gone through pretty much the entire weight saga: lose weight, gain weight, rebound, feel guilty, feel better, feel bad again… and on it goes. I used to be an athlete and from the age of seven I competed in athletics, endurance sports and dance events, and participated in galas. I always struggled with my weight and followed every new fad, from Weight Watchers and Slimming World to Rosemary Conley's *Fat Attack* and the Atkins Diet, from Mediterranean to low-carb to paleo to keto… to little long-term effect. To be honest, I got bored with all the food weighing and calorie counting. It was both exhausting and disheartening. I always felt like I was starving and, almost worse, missing out on the social 'involvement' of eating. Humans are social creatures, and any gathering tends to centre around food: meeting for coffee, evenings out, Christmas, birthdays, BBQs, and so on. It can feel miserable not joining in or constantly fussing about the calories on your plate.

What else was there left to do? Giving up wasn't an option because living optimised without chronic disease and feeling well remained my goals. I knew I needed muscle for energy reserves and the proper nutrition to prevent ageing. Mr H and his journey had taught me that. It was with great excitement and enthusiasm that I grabbed the opportunity to explore nutrigenomics.

Nutrigenomics

As explained in previous chapters, our DNA contains all the information our bodies need to build and define us. DNA determines how we function, how we grow and how we look. Genes are segments of DNA. We inherit our genes from our parents, and they define us as human beings by composing our cells in a unique way. Our genes instruct our bodies on how to behave. Genetics has become a central pillar of medicine and health in today's world. Genomics is the study of the composition of our specific genetic material (DNA and chromosomes) and can unlock our personal health risks – the risks hidden within our genes – replacing a one-size-fits-all model with specific diagnosis and management.

Nutrigenomics is the study of how food affects a person's genes and how a person's genes affect their body's responses to food. Discovering our personal nutrigenomics allows us to take an assertive, pro-active approach to preventing disease, instead of waiting for it to happen and then seeking treatment. If we really want to understand our body and what our genetics have in store for us, we can get the most accurate picture by analysing our DNA. It is the most reliable information available, and it is specific to the individual.

Nutrigenomics will provide information on how to optimise our diet with a series of nutritional alternatives. It relies on genetics to trigger effective treatment rather than merely following fad diets. Although the focus is not on weight loss but on healthy living, it can also support weight loss through a suggested balanced diet plan. Remember, our diet can actually change our DNA, resulting in ageing, followed by chronic disease.

Nutrigenetic testing

The idea behind nutrigenetic testing is to bring various specialists in the field together to optimise outcomes. The team consists of geneticists, immunologists, pharmacists and nutritionists. It is a one-off test requiring only a salivary sample obtained by swabbing the inside of your mouth (something we see on TV all the time in crime stories). There are a multitude of tests on the market but not all are as good or comprehensive and many are difficult to interpret. The Rolls Royce of nutrigenomic tests is produced by Fagron Genomics, the same company that developed the TeloTest discussed in the previous chapter. The test is available in some sixty countries around the world. It costs £550 and is offered by several UK clinics. It gives you a 360° overview of your genes and identifies risk factors associated with diet and food consumption. Before the DNA test is undertaken, body measurements and body form analysis are required, including a detailed history of food habits and supplements. This provides a comprehensive picture, which is then analysed in relation to fifteen 'macro DNA categories', as shown in the table below, producing specific predictions and recommendations.

**The fifteen macro categories
associated with weight loss and health**

DNA category	What the test investigates
Body form and structure	Your body's tendency to become overweight
Behavioural genetics in food intake	Your appetite and anxiety risk, which leads to increased dietary intake (or not)
Efficacy of physical exercise	Your endurance and the extent to which exercise will lower your cholesterol levels
Fat metabolism	Your response to fat intake – do you lose or gain fat because of your diet?
CHO (carbohydrate) metabolism	Your ability to digest starchy food – do you use it for energy or store it as fat?
Lipid (fat) metabolism	Your tendency towards increased triglycerides (a type of fat in the blood), leading to stroke and heart disease
Glucose metabolism	Your risk of increased glucose levels, leading to Type 2 diabetes
Flavour sensitivities	Your preference for sweet or savoury tastes

DNA category	What the test investigates
Toxic imbalances	How effectively your body eliminates poisons or pollutants
Supplementation problems	Excessive or inadequate levels of nutrients, such as calcium malabsorption, iron overload, low iron levels, excessive magnesium levels, abnormal selenium levels and sodium sensitivity
Intolerances	Whether your body is intolerant to substances such as lactose, caffeine or alcohol
Vitamin deficiencies	Whether you lack vitamins A, B, C, D or E and whether your body has the capability to make up deficiencies
Diet matching	How effective a diet such as low-calorie, low-fat or low-carbohydrate would be
Inflammation	Your body's immunity to viral, bacterial and parasitic infection, as well as autoimmune disorders
Hormones	The test measures hormones essential for energy balance and energy reserves and how they affect appetite and food intake stimulation

The results show your body's percentage efficacy in each area. From these results you will get a set of personalised diet recommendations (with a list of 800+ foods categorised according to how good or bad they are for you) and personalised nutrient recommendations, ie what supplements you need to take to optimise your well-being and prevent disease and injury.

Telomere testing

In Chapter 1, I introduced you to telomeres, the structures which protect our DNA against degradation and loss of genetic information, thereby protecting us against disease and degradation. Human telomeres shorten during the ageing process, but the speed of this process varies for each person. There is now a test that determines your telomere length and estimates the biological age of your cells known as a TeloTest. Knowing the condition of your telomeres and being able to track their shortening provides valuable information for improving and customising ageless therapies.

The test is performed in the same way as a nutrigenomic test, by taking a salivary sample from the inside of your mouth. It is new in the UK and only a few clinics currently perform it. The test compares the age of your cells with your real age and assesses how your body is doing at a cellular level. It then makes recommendations for keeping your lifestyle healthy, such as increasing your intake of foods with anti-inflammatory and antioxidant properties. The recommendations include lists of vitamins, amino acids, phytochemicals, antioxidants and minerals you should take to protect your telomeres against degradation.

Biohacking

Nutrigenomic and telomere testing are examples of the many technologies now available to us for improving our health and achieving wellness. Using such technologies is known as biohacking or DIY biology. Biohacking is a hybrid word coined from 'biology' and 'hacking' and has become synonymous with a fast-growing lifestyle involving all the things we humans do to enhance our appearance, our performance, our health and our wellbeing – in other words, to make ourselves look and feel better.

Biohacking has various aspects, including nutrition, supplements, hormonal treatments and the use of physical and electronic technology applications to track fitness, breathing, heart rate, sleep, calorie burning and fasting time. Its impacts can include improved memory, better focus and greater productivity, as well as self-fulfilment and happiness. It is not a new idea: humans have been doing DIY biology for a long time through yoga, meditation, exercise, sports, ice baths and all manner of dieting and dietary supplements, not to mention 'old' technology such as hearing aids, spectacles and contact lenses, pacemakers and other implants. The ultimate aim is to create an optimal self and enhance the quality of life through personalised and preventive measures.

One of the fastest-growing biohacking areas is personalised care and wellbeing to reduce the risk of chronic disease and ageing. The emphasis now is on preventive medicine, individual choice and the attainment of agelessness, rejecting the idea that the effects of ageing should be accepted as 'normal'. This is known as biomedicalisation.

Biomedicalisation moves away from disease classification and creates an optimal self, emphasising an individual approach to improve quality of life. It includes aesthetic services, balancing hormones and nutrition with the aim of achieving spiritual, sexual and emotional wellbeing. Rejecting a one-size-fits-all concept, it takes a holistic approach to quality of life and generates a personalised programme of health and wellness designed to prevent disease and age-related decline – the new goal of reversing ageing and extending health span.

One size does not fit all

The big lesson of the biohacking boom is that what works for one person does not necessarily work for another. We are all unique, with different genes, metabolisms, sensitivities and so on. Now that we have access to nutrigenomics, it makes sense to analyse our DNA to determine our body's unique needs accurately and then live accordingly.

My nutrigenetics test came back with a 106-page analysis and recommendations. The results were fascinating and created mixed feelings for me, fluctuating from anger and embarrassment (it seemed to be saying, 'I told you so') to relief and determination.

Two out of the twelve intolerance levels came back abnormal: for magnesium and salt. Low magnesium levels can cause headaches (which I seemed to have all the time) and nervousness; it can weaken bones and affect the heart. My calcium absorption was compromised by high levels of salt intake and genetic factors related to vitamin D, and my body had a faulty mechanism regarding salt excretion, which is usually through sweat and the kidneys. As a result I had a high sensitivity to salt, which meant my body retained it and it would eventually cause me hypertension, or high blood pressure, and could lead to heart disease.

The test also showed that I had low calcium and vitamin D levels despite supplementing throughout the year and making sure I spent enough time in the sun. This meant that I was at increased risk of osteoporosis and fractures, hair loss, tiredness, low immunity and much more.

As for my body weight, it revealed a medium to high risk of obesity and a high risk of rebound weight gain. My metabolic rate is medium to low, resulting in a slow weight loss capability and slow metabolism. I also tend to low satiety, which means that I rarely feel full, clearly explaining my constant hunger. After all these years I could now finally understand why it takes me ages to lose weight (and only by taking radical measures) and why doing so makes me feel unwell – because the diets I was imposing on my body were neither balanced nor sustainable. It was a relief to know it's my genetics, not me. No more self-flagellation.

The analysis suggested intensive dietary intervention as my best option. (I would have preferred exercise, but hey ho.) So, what kind of intervention did I need?

Here came another shocker. The diet I'd most enjoyed was the keto diet. Its principles are high fats, moderate protein and low carbs. A nutritionist recommended this diet and the research around it made a lot of sense. I also found that it worked better, which meant that I enjoyed it a lot more. However, my analysis showed that I have a highly ineffective fat-burning capacity and recommended that I decrease my fat intake significantly, as I would derive no benefit from it and it would not help improve my HDL levels – high-density lipoprotein being the type of fat that mops up cholesterol and other fats that clog arteries.

I had a medium to high risk of dysregulation regarding carbohydrates, which meant that my body readily stored carbs as fat and was at increased risk of developing high cholesterol and diabetes. The analysis recommended that I urgently eliminate refined carbohydrates and move to wholegrain, but in low quantities. Unfortunately, this also meant that I was at a high risk of Type 2 diabetes and a medium to high risk of insulin resistance. The good news was that my fat metabolism was in excellent shape, an efficient fat metabolism being a good thing, as HDL and triglycerides are the usual culprits in stroke.

As for antioxidant capabilities – a body's capacity to clear toxins caused by free radicals[21] – my body was severely compromised: catechol-O-methyltransferase (COMT) enzymes were compromised, resulting in additional risk of severe cellular damage. The nerve cells in our bodies produce COMT enzymes, which are a methylation enzyme, responsible for proper formation of DNA. Defective methylation can lead to the build-up of toxins. To prevent further cellular damage my DNA report recommended ginseng, turmeric and green tea. Other treatment recommendations are magnesium and vitamin B supplements, especially vitamins B2, B6, B9 and B12. I was recommended SAMe supplements, a product then utterly unknown to me. S-adenosyl-L-methionine is a compound found naturally in the body. It helps produce and regulate hormones and maintain cell membranes. It is recommended for a variety of illnesses and ailments, including depression, anxiety, heart disease, fibromyalgia, abdominal pain, osteoarthritis, bursitis, tendonitis, chronic lower back pain, dementia, Alzheimer's disease, chronic fatigue syndrome, memory loss, liver disease and Parkinson's disease – as well as to slow the ageing process.

The final part of the test consists of diet recommendations and supplementation advice from nutritional experts. They determined that I was severely deficient in vitamins B6 and E and advised me that calorie counting was of no use to me. Instead, I should start a mixed nutritional plan low in carbohydrates for the best metabolic balance in my body. I received a comprehensive list of over 800 foods categorised into green, yellow, amber and red. Red foods should be restricted to small quantities and frequency, whereas green foods are always allowed.

I was astounded by my test results. They told me things about my body that nobody could know, including my doctor, and what to take to improve my outcomes. For example, I could immediately reduce my salt intake to prevent hypertension. Like most people of my age, I was starting to experience 'ageing' effects, such as pain in my feet after a long day, stiffness getting up in the morning, and brain fog (being unable to think clearly). Knowing the exact nutrition I required to improve my symptoms was both heartening and exciting. My newfound knowledge about my body's needs and how it worked meant that I finally had a roadmap that would avoid damage to my body, eventually resulting in ageing and chronic disease, and take me towards wellbeing.

I can now nourish my body accurately and save money instead of wasting it on products my body doesn't need or cannot use while also treating the areas where I experience symptoms with the correct vitamins.

Summary

Thanks to modern technology, we can now biohack ourselves to optimise our health and prevent cellular injury and ageing. Nutrigenomics, TeloTest and the DNA TrichoTest are not yet the panacea for ageing, but they are inching us closer to agelessness and giving us hope.

7

The Dreaded Menopause

Few areas of health have caused more myths, debates or misunderstandings than the menopause (in women; andropause in men). As you now know, we need strong muscles, correct nourishment and precise supplementation to thrive and live well. Unfortunately, this is not enough, especially for women and especially when they reach the menopause.

'Menopause' originates from the Greek words *menos* (month) and *pausis* (pause), and means 'monthly pauses' – in other words the cessation of monthly periods. It is the stage in life when our reproductive system retires. It is a natural physiological phenomenon caused by programmed cell death. Anyone who has ovaries cannot escape menopause. As a species we outlive our fertility, and most women will spend more than a third of their life beyond menopause. Interestingly, it also happens in the animal kingdom – but only in elephants and killer and short-finned pilot whales (a useless fact, but one that makes me smile).

The role of hormones in ageing

Since antiquity, humans have recognised that declining hormone levels affects their sexual performance and energy. The ancient Greeks, Egyptians and Indians tried to compensate by ingesting animal testes.[22] We are now better informed about the causes and effects of hormonal decline. We realise that it accounts for many age-related diseases, such as cardiovascular disease, osteoporosis and cancers. It is responsible for age-associated symptoms such as hair and muscle loss, fatigue, increased body fat and cognitive defects such as brain fog, memory loss and depression. Chronic diseases multiply dramatically within a short period in midlife women due to menopause.[23]

The functions of hormones reach far beyond their most common association with ovulation, pregnancy and sex drive. Hormones are chemical messengers that travel throughout the body, coordinating complex processes like growth, metabolism and fertility to ensure our survival. Hormonal imbalances can impact virtually every major system and organ in the body and can have a significant impact on quality of life.

Hormone functions fall into two categories: anabolic (to build tissue) and catabolic (to break down tissue). Anabolic hormones are testosterone, dehydroepi-androsterone (DHEA), oestrogen and progesterone, whose function is to keep us youthful by (re)building our tissues. (Anabolic hormones are also called hormones of youth, sex hormones, steroid hormones and sex steroids.) Catabolic hormones, such as cortisol, break down tissues during stress and anxiety, as we have seen. In this chapter we are concerned with anabolic sex hormones, which are affected by menopause.

When our ovary factory shuts down, we no longer make oestrogen – the hormone that regulates a woman's fertility. This causes changes to pretty much everything – from our hair to our feet. Depleted oestrogen particularly affects the skin, resulting in dryness, fine wrinkling and poor healing. The amount of collagen in our skin can reduce by up to 30%, affecting our elastin, or skin elasticity.

There is also an effect on the extracellular matrix (the tissue just under the second layer of skin), which contains collagen, fibroblasts, glycosaminoglycans (GAGs) and hyaluronic acid. The purpose of GAGs is to draw water into the skin, providing cushioning within the skin to protect it against turgor, or compression, and give it suppleness. The purpose of hyaluronic acid is to retain water and keep tissue well lubricated and moist.

The reduction in progesterone increases the impact of androgens (a group of hormones that play a role in male traits), which impacts the sebaceous glands, which lubricate and produce oil in the skin. The skin and hair can become oilier, which can impact hair either by miniaturisation of the hair follicles, resulting in hair loss, or by increasing vellus hair (fine baby hair on the face) to thick mature hair, which is why some women start to grow facial hair. In extreme cases women can grow a full beard and moustache. Lack of oestrogen and progesterone explains why mature women can suddenly develop acne, enlarged pores, oily skin and unwanted facial hair.

Bones

Bone growth continues into adulthood and most people achieve a peak bone mass in the spine and hip by their mid-twenties. Other bones reach a peak around the age of forty, then their bone mass starts to decline. Our genetics determine our peak bone mass but generally, by the time we hit seventy, our bone mass has decreased by between 30% and 40%. For bone to remain dense and healthy, it requires continuous remodelling. This is called the bone turnover cycle. The principal factors that regulate bone formation and growth are the hormones oestrogen and parathyroid (also called parathormone or parathyrin), vitamin D3 and calcium, and exercise.

Because oestrogen plays a significant role in bone development, when a woman reaches menopause her bone turnover cycle becomes severely impaired. The amount of bone resorbed outweighs the amount deposited. Bone becomes weak and brittle, symptoms of osteoporosis. The primary health threat from osteoporosis is fractures, which may lead to loss of mobility and independence and affect quality of life. Even if we sail through menopause and the symptoms appear to be over, the effects will still be ongoing, especially those that affect the density of our bone and muscle, which we desperately need if we are to avoid sarcopenia. Sarcopenia is loss of muscle mass, resulting in loss of energy and reduced functionality, compounding into frailty associated with ageing.

Three significant stages

Menopause is a process rather than an event – the average duration of menopausal symptoms is seven years, but for some women symptoms continue for the rest of their lives – and three stages can be identified:

1. **Perimenopause:** A common misconception is that menopause starts a year before it takes full effect, generally around the age of fifty. It is imperative to understand that menopause can begin as early as your mid-thirties or during your forties. In this first stage, your ovaries are figuring out how to retire and you will experience some or all of the symptoms listed below.

2. **Menopause:** Menopause proper means that you have gone twelve months without a period. Initially, you might experience sadness or a sense of bereavement or loss. Your womanhood as you know it has come to an end, although you still have many years ahead of you. Some or all of the symptoms listed below may still occur during this stage and can continue for as long as ten years.

3. **Postmenopause:** You have come through the other side, and most of your symptoms have disappeared. You may have regained your energy and feel normal again. However, you still have low oestrogen, which means high risks of osteoporosis, heart disease and changes to your vagina and bladder (see below). It is imperative to protect your bones during this stage.

Symptoms

There are two types of symptoms: physical and psychological. Some of the most common are described below.

Physical

During perimenopause, our bodies produce less oestrogen; fertility decreases, and conceiving becomes more difficult or impossible. Women may experience some or all of the following physical symptoms:

- Periods that are lighter, shorter and further apart, or heavier, longer and more frequent, or any combination of these at different times

- Hot flushes and sweats (vasomotor symptoms) – the most common symptom reported by women in perimenopause – which result because decreased oestrogen levels cause the hypothalamus (the body's thermostat) to become more sensitive to slight changes in body temperature

- Night sweats

- Palpitations

- Fluctuations in blood pressure

- Migraine

- Urogenital symptoms such as vaginal dryness, itching, pain during intercourse and urinary incontinence

- Bone and joint pains, especially in the hips

- Muscle twitching and cramps

- Tremors or uncontrolled shaking

- Delayed or slow movement due to the associated aches and cramps in bone and muscle

- Disturbed sleep – caused by hot flushes and sweats

- Breast tenderness

- Hair loss

- Skin ageing

- Many women complain of symptoms similar to those of fibromyalgia, a chronic disease, the cause of which is unknown. Sadly, these women are often prescribed painkillers and antidepressants. I have found in practice that once we have restored the hormone deficit, these symptoms disappear.

Psychological

The lack of oestrogen may decrease the production of the neurotransmitter serotonin and reduce the number of serotonin receptors in the brain. It also modifies the production and the effects of endorphins, the brain's feel-good chemicals. Anxiety, anger and depression are common during perimenopause, and the last of these can reach dangerous levels. Other psychological symptoms include:

- Irritability

- Mood swings

- Unexplained anger, sadness or unreasonable behaviour

- Depression – in severe cases, this can lead the person to feel suicidal

- Poor concentration

- Memory loss or 'brain fog' – oestrogen controls brain development so, as levels decrease, we may experience confusion, an inability to concentrate or memory loss

- Tiredness

- Loss of confidence

Menopause symptoms are complex, and women's experiences vary greatly. Some sail through menopause with minimal discomfort, while others experience debilitating symptoms. In GP practice, I have known women to cry, telling me how 'evil' they have become, with uncharacteristic outbursts of anger and personality changes, which can affect their partners and family as well as themselves. It is important to remember that even if you escape some of the worst symptoms, you cannot avoid the impact of the reduction in oestrogen production. Even though some sail through menopause with few symptoms, the loss of hormones greatly impacts the whole body and its tissues, with effects such as muscle wasting, osteoporosis, and loss of collagen in skin and other tissues.

Menopausal symptoms can last from six months to two years or up to ten years. It is a long time to feel miserable. As your quality of life diminishes, your body weakens physically and your risk of disease increases.

The silent condition

Most women are only too happy to discuss hot flushes and mood swings, but they are less willing to talk about other symptoms of menopause. This is particularly true of vulvovaginal atrophy (VVA), which women are often reluctant even to recognise despite the fact that over 50% experience the symptoms.

The lack of oestrogen during menopause not only causes vaginal skin tissue to become thin but also affects the mucosa (inner layer of the vagina), affecting its elasticity and reducing the inner folds that allow for distention, leading to shortening and narrowing of the vagina, and even the muscular structure of the pelvic floor, urethra (urinary opening) and bladder, leading to mechanical weakness. These changes lead to vaginal dryness, itching, irritation and burning, vaginismus (tightening of vaginal muscles resulting in pain during penetration), making intercourse painful (a condition known as dyspareunia) and even leading to vaginal bleeding post-intercourse. Other symptoms include increased urinary frequency and urgency, dysuria (burning, tingling or stinging when passing urine) and urinary infections. The labia themselves become discoloured, thin and sensitive to touch when wiping after ablutions.

VVA also causes reduced female sexual function, leading to distress, pain, a drop in desire and lack of arousal, pleasure or orgasm. Experiencing sexual dysfunction creates anxiety, which causes disturbance in the brain, affecting the bioavailability of luteinising hormone, further reducing the sex drive – a vicious circle. While most menopausal symptoms resolve after a while (months to years), VVA is chronic and progressive.

Despite all this, women remain largely silent about VVA. Whereas erectile dysfunction has emerged as one of men's most prominent sexual health concerns, with a worldwide prevalence ranging from 13% to 28% of men aged forty to eighty,[24] women rarely report their discomfort or seek treatment, despite the fact that over 50% of us experience these symptoms, which can be devastating if they remain untreated. Many women experience shame and would rather avoid embarrassment, preferring to dismiss their feelings as a 'normal' part of ageing, despite the evidence that many women are still sexually active later in life.

Another impact of menopause that even medical books and other literature on the subject are often silent on is how many women become suicidal during menopause. Recent programmes to raise awareness of menopause have created a dialogue among my patients and staff. The majority admitted to suicidal thoughts and even admission to psychiatric wards and sectioning. They were too ashamed to admit these things 'in public', or concerned that they would upset their families.

ADAM – the male menopause

What is not widely known is that men also experience a kind of menopause. This is commonly known as 'andro-pause', but the term is misleading because men do not suddenly stop having periods and, unlike menopause, the phenomenon does not happen to all men. A more appropriate term applicable to men is androgen decline in the ageing male (ADAM), which I use here.

In contrast to the abrupt hormonal change in women, the male hormone known as testosterone remains relatively constant until around aged fifty, when it starts to fall gradually. Along with this decline goes that of the production of growth hormones (which in fact decreases by 14% each decade after puberty). This is associated with changes in lean muscle mass, bone density and hair distribution, and contributes to an obesity pattern of large breasts and abdomen.

Like women, men suffer a range of physical and emotional symptoms associated with ADAM, which include:

- Mood swings, irritability and anger

- Erectile dysfunction and diminished sexual desire

- Decreased intellectual activity

- Reduced three-dimensional observation (the illusion of depth)

- Loss of lean body mass and the ability to exercise due to reduced muscle volume and strength

- Fat redistribution, causing the development of a large belly or gynaecomastia ('man boobs' or moobs)

- A general lack of enthusiasm or energy and increased tiredness

- Insomnia

- Poor concentration and short-term memory

- Depression

- Hair loss and skin changes

- Decrease in bone mineral density, resulting in osteoporosis

I have been working in medicine for thirty years but only came across discussions of ADAM while researching and writing this book. Why is this? Allegedly it is because there is a stigma attached to male menopause. There is also disagreement, even among those in the healthcare industry, as to whether male menopause exists at all. In fact, ADAM tends to occur in older men with heart disease, obesity, high blood pressure and Type 2 diabetes. Other underlying lifestyle factors include lack of exercise, smoking, alcohol consumption, stress, anxiety and sleep deprivation.

The association with testosterone is also unclear. Some older men still have high levels of testosterone but experience symptoms. Men are also affected by other hormonal decline, which I will discuss within the hormonal treatment recommendations in the next chapter.

Summary

Menopause and ADAM are processes rather than sudden events, and the symptoms can continue for the rest of our lives. Understanding the underlying causes of these symptoms and how they affect us is essential to any treatment programme.

8

Menopause Treatment – HRT Vs BHRT

Despite the fact menopause is common and expected, there is a persistent problem in practice. Menopausal symptoms are often misdiagnosed as fibromyalgia, depression, arthritis, thyroid disease or 'just ageing', leaving women feeling even more debilitated. In GP practice, I have found that many women who experience menopausal symptoms such as emotional outbursts, changes within themselves and low moods are pre-scribed antidepressants or referred to organisations like Let's Talk for cognitive behavioural therapy. Some GP practices flatly refuse to treat patients for meno-pause (though others are highly proactive). The problem is that there is little training and no uni-formity or consistency in managing menopausal women in a GP practice.

Fortunately, there has recently been a fundamental shift towards preventing age-related decline, and one of the approaches is to replace hormones whose levels decline with age. In her book *Ageless: The naked truth about bioidentical hormones*,[25] Suzanne Somers argues that hormone imbalance should not be taken lightly, as it can lead to us losing our grip on feeling normal.

Hormone management is vital not only to alleviate the symptoms of menopause, but also to prevent ageing.

There are various methods of hormone management, the most widely used and best-known being hormone replacement therapy (HRT).

HRT

HRT uses synthetic and therefore not naturally occurring hormones that have a different chemical structure and composition than the hormones produced within our body (some synthetic hormones are derived from horse urine) but are chemically altered to mimic oestrogen. They are not in fact hormone replacements but hormone substitutes. It is important to note that a small change to a chemical structure can make a huge difference in function. It is no wonder that HRT frequently makes headlines claiming that it is the most significant cause of breast cancer and carries risks of heart disease, stroke and blood clots. These are countered by claims that the trials from which those conclusions are drawn are invalid. The debate is ongoing and continually rears its head.

A myriad of studies has been performed over the years, but they are disjointed because most examine single issues in isolation. An example is a study conducted by orthopaedics investigating fractures and how to avoid them in menopausal women.[26] On the other hand, cardiologists examine the menopausal impact on the heart but do not consider osteoporosis when they make their recommendations. Oncologists will research the effect of oestrogen on breast cancer, neglecting the importance of mental, heart or bone health. The various research outcomes lead to confusion in practice. Few studies take the time to truly understand how devastating menopause is on the body and mind of women.

From the point of view of the practitioner who has to decide whether or not to prescribe hormone treatment for menopause, the disparity is concerning because no one wants to be responsible for causing harm. Trying to interpret the studies and determine if it is safe or not is like walking through a minefield.

There is, however, light at the end of the tunnel in the form of an alternative treatment: bioidentical hormone replacement therapy (BHRT).

BHRT

The symptoms of hormone-related conditions can be treated with BHRT and nutritional supplements. BHRT is the use of bioidentical hormones to replace and rebalance the body's hormones during the changes leading up to menopause and beyond. The leader in the field by a large margin is Marion Gluck, who runs a clinic in London and with whom I trained in BHRT.

BHRT is different from HRT because a bioidentical hormone has the exact same chemical and molecular structure as the naturally occurring hormone that is produced within the body.[27] This means that the bioidentical replacement treatment fits the hormone receptors better and therefore causes fewer side effects than synthetic hormones and is better tolerated.

The hormonal blood tests required for BHRT include testosterone, oestrogen, progesterone, DHEA, cholesterol and vitamin D. In men, an additional test consists of a prostate antigen to ensure that there is no risk of testicular cancer when considering prescribing testosterone. In the context of ageing, we are concerned principally with oestrogen, progesterone, testosterone and DHEA.

The blood test results are different for each individual, who will experience a unique set of symptoms based on their specific hormone levels. Knowing your specific blood levels allows specialists to prescribe the hormones you need – a truly tailor-made treatment.

The benefits of oestrogen

Oestrogen is responsible for the formation and growth of breast tissue and ovulation. It regulates cardiovascular function, bone mass, development and the cognitive functions of memory and learning, explaining why women experience memory problems and 'brain fog' when they start perimenopause. Both females and males produce oestrogen, but women make more of it.

The functions of oestrogen are:

- Regulating body temperature

- Promoting healthy sleep

- Increasing blood flow

- Maintaining memory

- Enhancing concentration

- Decreasing wrinkles

- Muscle maintenance

- Maintaining artery elasticity and preventing heart disease

- Maintaining collagen levels in the skin preventing ageing, which changes when oestrogen stops in menopause

- Maintaining the thickness of the vaginal wall

- Improving mood

- Increasing libido

- Lowering the risk of colon cancer

- Maintaining bone density, which prevents osteoporosis

- Cleaning up free radicals

The benefits of progesterone

Progesterone plays a significant role in the menstrual function and early pregnancy. The functions of progesterone are:

- Reducing hot flushes

- Maintaining the endometrium (the lining of the uterus)

- Acting as a natural diuretic

- Acting as a natural antidepressant

- Helping normalise blood sugar levels

- Restoring proper cell oxygen levels

- Improving cholesterol levels

- Protecting the breast against fibrocystic disease

- Helping the body to use fat for energy

- Helping thyroid action[28]

- Restoring libido

- Normalising zinc and copper levels

- Protecting against endometrial (uterine) cancer

- Stimulating bone building

- Improving energy, stamina and endurance

- Maintaining muscle mass

The benefits of testosterone

Testosterone is a sex hormone and an anabolic steroid. Although it is typically considered a male hormone, women also produce testosterone, but in smaller amounts. Testosterone:

- Increases muscle mass and strength

- Increases sexual function

- Increases confidence, motivation and energy

- Increases bone density

- Improves memory

- Improves mood and vitality

- Increases the ability to grow body hair

DHEA – 'the cure-all for ageing'

DHEA is an evolutionary hormone made in the brain that promotes neuronal (brain) growth and regeneration. It is also the most abundant steroid hormone. DHEA undergoes a series of chemical reactions, collectively termed 'the steroid hormone cascade', which is how other hormones are made. In simple terms, cholesterol makes pregnenolone, which makes DHEA, which in turn makes oestrogen and testosterone. This means that if our DHEA declines, our oestrogen and progesterone decline with it. Levels begin to decrease after the age of thirty, at a rate of around 2% per year. Women lose about half their DHEA by the age of forty-five.

The drop in DHEA correlates with signs and symptoms associated with ageing, including depression, diminished cognition, malignancy in general, decreased bone mineral density, arthritis, reduced libido in women, congestive heart failure and increased mortality in men. A decline in DHEA results in a decrease in wellbeing, and various publications[29] report that supplementing DHEA has the following benefits:

- Increases quality of life

- Boosts the immune system

- Helps us deal with stress

- Improves memory

- Increases strength

- Protects against diabetes

- Increases energy levels

- Helps with weight loss

- Reduces joint pain

- Alleviates symptoms of fatigue

- Enhances libido

- Improves erectile function and increases sexual desire and intercourse satisfaction

- Has anti-ageing properties

Sadly, menopause and andropause are poorly understood in GP practice and DHEA is not even tested, acknowledged or understood by many in practice. It was not until I studied with Marion Gluck that I came across the purpose and function of DHEA and its subsequent hormonal cascade. Because DHEA is the 'mother hormone' of oestrogen and testosterone, in some cases fixing DHEA can naturally improve oestrogen and testosterone without having to prescribe further hormonal supplements.

How BHRT works

BHRT acts differently from traditional HRT and has different effects. Whereas HRT is synthetic, BHRT is natural or human-identical. Bioidentical steroid hormones are not in fact human in origin, but their behaviour and function are identical to those of human hormones. BHRT derives from a plant oil called diosgenin that derives from soybean and wild yams, has a 100% identical structure to our hormones and is specifically formulated according to our unique blood profile.

Most of my patients report feeling better within a couple of days of starting BHRT, with more energy and improved general wellbeing. The following two cases are typical.

Case study: Anita

Anita was forty-eight and had had two complicated pregnancies with continued heavy bleeding, resulting in a hysterectomy at thirty. Her life had been miserable for the past twelve years. Her symptoms included dizziness, tingling in her fingers and toes, constipation, extreme vaginal dryness resulting in painful intercourse, extreme tiredness, illness and chronic pain in her hips and feet. She had had two spontaneous fractures in each foot and gained a substantial amount of weight; she had also started to lose her hair. She described symptoms of muscle pain and sluggish movement due to body pain, and lumps and bumps in her body that were painful to touch. These, she had been told, were caused by excess toxins in her body. Her life had changed significantly, and she felt that she had lost her old self.

Where she lived, no doctors believed in HRT and advised her to accept all this as 'a woman's lot'; so she came to me for help. When I saw her, I was shocked. Most of her weight was distributed over her abdomen and down her legs, which looked like tree trunks because of retained fluid. The skin on her face had thickened unevenly and was discoloured, with ingrowing hair, and the skin around her vagina had become so thin that it was even painful for her to urinate. She had bouts of incontinence, her ears were ringing and she had started to lose teeth. She was breathless on minimum exertion, she felt increasingly anxious for no apparent reason (unusual for her) and felt muddled, often forgetting where she was driving or what she was doing.

Her blood test results showed small red blood cells, which explained her breathlessness, and deficient vitamin B12. Vitamin B12 helps form red blood cells but it also affects the central nervous system, which explained the tingling sensation in her hands. Vitamin B12 has many functions, and correcting her deficiency resulted in rapid improvements to many of her symptoms.

Anita also had low vitamin D levels despite supplementing. Low vitamin D causes fatigue, bone weakness (explaining the multitude of fractures), joint and muscle pain, low energy, low mood and anxiety, and increases the likelihood of illness.

Anita's treatment plan consisted of first restoring her vitamin B12 and D levels.

Anita also had a borderline thyroid problem that could have been the cause of her constipation, which meant that she was recirculating toxins, which in turn created additional stress on her body. Most concerning were her hormone levels. She was deficient in oestrogen, testosterone and DHEA, and she had raised cholesterol levels, which were impacting her body negatively. If we could fix her hormones, we would also fix her cholesterol and, no doubt, improve her quality of life. Considering the hormonal evidence, the benefits would far outweigh the risks.

Anita's prescription consisted of DHEA, oestrogen and progesterone. DHEA would combat ageing effects, reduce anxiety, stress and joint pain, increase her energy levels, improve her memory and enhance her libido while also alleviating other menopausal symptoms. DHEA could also help her with weight loss.

The aims of giving Anita oestrogen were to improve her blood flow and hopefully improve her legs, which were so pale and cold. Oestrogen also produces collagen, which should help with her fine lines and wrinkles as well as her osteoporosis. Oestrogen helps clear up free radicals, which can help with the toxicity caused by ongoing constipation and simultaneously reduce the risk of heart disease.

Progesterone is a natural diuretic and would hopefully help alleviate oedema in her legs and restore proper oxygen levels while normalising her blood sugar levels. Progesterone also improves cholesterol levels and maintains muscle mass, which would improve her stamina, energy and endurance. Progesterone normalises zinc and copper levels, which are significant for hair growth and cell function, and uses fat for energy – another aid to weight loss. Finally, progesterone reduces hot flushes and is a natural antidepressant.

Both oestrogen and progesterone enhance libido, improve mood and maintain memory.

Restoring Anita's hormonal balance meant that we had paused ageing and staved off age-related disease. We had started to reverse the impact her hormonal imbalance was having on her life. After treatment, she reported a general feeling of wellbeing, more brain clarity and stamina, weight loss and firmer muscles. The toxic lumps on her arms and legs cleared, she was opening her bowels more regularly and had reduced urinary problems. Vaginally she seemed to be less dry, and she had an improved libido. Anita's skin started looking better, and the hair growth on her chin had been reduced. She was feeling better every day, achieving significant improvements within three months. She was only forty-eight. Imagine what her life would have been like at fifty-eight or sixty-eight if she had simply accepted her condition as a 'woman's lot'.

Case study: Ginny

Ginny was a forty-eight-year-old mother, wife, student and practice manager in a flourishing progressive clinic. She presented with symptoms typical of menopause but had been diagnosed with fibromyalgia. She was tired and brain fogged with increased visceral fat around her abdomen, aches, pains and low mood, verging on severe depression. She also suffered reduced immunity and always seemed to have a cold or similar symptoms. Her symptoms had been going on for five years with no relief. She had refused to take the antidepressants prescribed by her doctor along with painkillers. She felt that they made her feel worse: more listless with a negative outlook. She had recently had a frozen shoulder and had to have physiotherapy treatment. She often complained of sleepless nights caused by the shoulder pain and, although the physiotherapy had had some effect, she still had minimal movement in the shoulder. She struggled to regulate her body temperature, constantly feeling hot and getting severe flushes.

Ginny's test results came back with low oestrogen, progesterone, DHEA and vitamin D. Within a week of starting BHRT, she had increased energy and brain clarity, and no shoulder pain. She had a full range of movement back in her shoulder and better sleep, with improved results daily. Ginny had struggled with her weight, especially around her abdomen, and no exercise or diet had made much of a difference. Since she started taking hormones, her body fat had been reducing. Her overall health and wellbeing had improved. She was getting her life back and enjoying it.

Hormonal balance is essential for our bodies, which need appropriate amounts of hormones. However, each human is individual, which means that they each have different hormone deficiencies and therefore require individualised treatments. BHRT is unique in this sense because its formulations can be made specific to an individual based on their hormonal imbalance. This process is known as compounding. Compounding refers to individualised formulations developed by specialist pharmacists working within detailed, well-researched guidelines to produce pure pharmaceutical-grade hormonal formulations.

Testosterone replacement

Testosterone replacement therapy is associated with increased libido, improved erectile function, increased androgen-sensitive hair growth, increased lean body mass and decreased fat mass. It also increases bone mineral density and strength. Trials in testosterone replacement have shown a statistically significant increase in the number of satisfying sexual events per month, decreased personal distress and increased arousal, pleasure and self-image. If men have normal testosterone but experience other symptoms, they need further exploration of their hormones.

Summary

I have argued throughout this book that every person is unique, with unique needs, and that one size does not fit all. The same goes for hormone testing and treatment. Every patient receiving treatment will respond differently and experience different benefits or side effects; these will therefore need to be closely monitored, and the doses adapted accordingly. Prescribing hormones for deficiency syndromes should be as natural as possible, and studies indicate that BHRT is safe and effective.

Part Three

LOOKING AND FEELING YOUR BEST

The majority of the patients I have interviewed seek treatments because, at their core, they are experiencing change. The changes occur in the family setting (as children leave home), socially and at work. My patients are either at the pinnacle of their careers, starting to consider retirement or embarking on something new. Physical changes are also occurring – to the bones, hair and face, where the stresses and strains of life are beginning to make themselves visible: lines are deepening, cheeks sagging, jowls developing, wrinkles forming and skin dulling. We don't recover as quickly as before and have newfound aches and pains, less muscle and less energy. Some of us are even beginning to experience signs of chronic disease.

People attend my clinic seeking aesthetic treatments to look a fresher and better version of themselves. Many hope that if they look better, they will feel better. To some extent this works, but it is short-lived because unless the whole of the ageing process is addressed, it will rapidly progress.

The aesthetic industry is perpetuating this problem. Most aesthetic clinics offer treatments for facial rejuvenation and hair loss, including fat reduction and skin rejuvenation. They miss the point that the challenge to age less involves hormones, supplements and nutrition, as well as a multisystem approach on the outside.

The crux of the problem with the aesthetic market is that the causes of ageing are not fully explained, so that patients don't understand the reasons for the anatomical changes to their face and put their trust in practitioners to provide them with a 'miracle' cure. The following chapters aim to inform you and give you the most relevant and up-to-date knowledge so that you can make better decisions about how you look and feel, about your health and wellbeing.

9

How And Why
Our Faces Change

Every sunrise brings about changes to our face in subtle ways, but the mind's eye remembers the last image of a face, which is why we hardly notice these small daily changes in ourselves; we only become aware of them when looking at old photos. If we don't see someone for a year or more, we can be shocked by how much their appearance has changed.

The first signs of facial ageing become apparent between the ages of twenty and thirty, resulting in changes to skin texture and soft tissue, lines and bony prominence. As time marches on, we experience facial volume loss and progressive bone resorption (caused by menopause, bearing children, nutrition, disease, stress, trauma and injury) and a further combination of decreased tissue elasticity and redistribution of fat pads. The reasons for this are a motion in our facial bones caused by contraction, changes in bone density and bone resorption. Bone resorption is much more profound in women than men due to the flux in our hormones caused by childbearing and menopause.

What we may not realise is that our whole face changes at every anatomic level due to the complex interplay between the facial muscles and their repetitive internal and external activity. The onset and speed of these changes are different for each structure and vary between individuals as well as between ethnic groups. Skeletal changes, for example, occur much more in our face than the other bones in our body. The process is dynamic because it affects not only the bone but also the fat pads overlying the bone, which slide down due to gravity, facial ligament laxity or fat pad degeneration.

Facial attributes

Reading and understanding facial expressions is a part of social interaction and social intelligence and part of human evolution and anthropology. Facial expressions signal nonverbal communication, and there are basic emotional expressions that are universal, such as disgust, fear, joy, surprise, anger and sadness. Specific muscles are involved in specific facial expressions; for example, the corrugator muscles between the eyes create a frown, and raised eyebrows are caused by the frontalis muscle on the forehead.

While a downturned mouth signals negative emotions such as disapproval or unhappiness, an upturned mouth indicates joy or happiness. A clenched jaw or teeth signals potentially worsening anger, conveying a sense of danger. When we meet a person for the first time, we automatically scan their facial features, starting at their eyes and then dropping to their mouth, searching for telltale signs of their mood and ensuring that we are safe to be near them. Another person's face can also affect us sensually. Scientists have found that the size of somebody's lips plays a key role in determining whether they are sexually attractive to other people. Full lips are accepted as sexually more attractive than thin lips, which is why many people, particularly women, seek aesthetic treatment that can enhance their lips.

Most patients attending my clinic do so because they have assigned a particular meaning to their facial attributes. Most common is that they look sad or tired when they don't feel that way. This is usually due to the loss of fat pads in the face. Many women, especially grandmothers, seek treatments because of their grandchildren. They say that their grandchildren frequently ask them why they are so disapproving, or that they fear them because of their permanent frown line.

The important thing I have discovered is that every person is unique, and their feelings and requirements are different.

Case study: Georgina

Georgina was fifty-seven when she came to me for treatment. Her life journey etched on her face contributed to facial attributes of tiredness and sadness.

Her eyes had lost their sparkle, her skin was dull, and she looked beaten and unhappy within herself. We will be returning to Georgina's story in later chapters. First, I will delve a little deeper into the facial changes that can come with ageing and how they are caused.

Shifting layers

Our face, scalp and neck are constructed of five layers. Each layer also relates to a structure within that layer. When I assess a face, I follow an outside-in process, reflecting on each layer and the problem associated with it.

The first layer to consider is the skin. I deliberate on any changes to the skin, such as lines, wrinkles, colour, texture, scars, pigmentation, lentigines (age spots) and laxity, and then visualise and consider the connective tissue in the second layer, also known as the extra-cellular matrix (ECM). ECM provides the structural scaffold in our face and consists of collagen and elastin, fat cells and fibroblasts. It also regulates cell growth and behaviour. UV radiation, nutrition and ageing all impact our ECM, reducing the 'plumpness' of our skin and making it less like a stretched canvas. Reduced elasticity causes the skin to fold in on itself and develop deep and superficial lines.

The third layer is the musculoaponeurotic layer, where the muscles that control facial expression and move-ment are located. Changes in the tension of these muscles, combined with reduced collagen, contribute to lines, wrinkles and phenomena such as the downward turned mouth (the 'resting bitch face') and hooding of the eyelid.

Beneath the muscles is another layer, known as the loose areolar connective tissue. This tissue is a mesh of collagen, elastic tissue and fibres, and deep fat connecting the underlying tissue and the superficial tissue, holding the face together. With ageing, this tissue weakens and shifts, causing the most significant changes to the structure and features of the face.

Deep fat exists in specific compartments that further contribute to facial features. The loss in these compartments caused by resorption and changing bone result in peaks and troughs (mountains and valleys) in the face and is the main reason patients seek treatments for specific areas such as cheeks, chin or jawline. Most of my treatments take place within these compartments or on the bones below to restore the lost facial features.

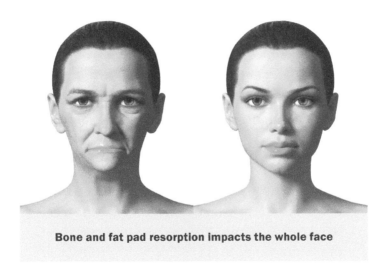

Bone and fat pad resorption impacts the whole face

The fifth and final layer of the face is its bony features. The bony component of the face is vital for its three-dimensional contours as it provides the scaffolding or framework over which the soft tissues such as our fat pads and muscles are draped. The combination of bone and tissue that scaffolds the face determines its shape.

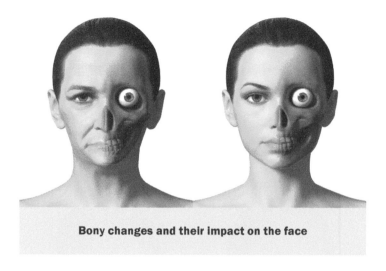

Bony changes and their impact on the face

The skeletal changes that occur in our face as we age are:

- The dome of our skull shrinks, getting smaller, which impacts the muscles in the forehead. The muscles are less stretched and perform a bit like a slack rope, creating undulations in the skin and sagging.

- Our forehead moves forwards and downwards.

- The lateral orbit, or outer angles of our eyes, expands outwards, increasing the eye size and creating a 'hollowness' within the eye.

- The supraorbital ridges, or bony ridges above the eyes, expand outwards becoming more prominent, especially in men.

- The glabella, or bone between our eyes, protrudes.

- Our cheekbones decrease in height and move backwards so that our face starts to 'fall in on itself'.

- The width of our nose increases, causing the tip of the nose to rotate downwards, resulting in a classic 'witch's nose'.

- Our jaw shortens in length and height, causing the tip of the chin to become blunter and turn upwards, as well as the dreaded 'turkey neck'.

The changes to the bony structure shift the skin's tension, resulting in deeper nasolabial folds and changes around our mouth. The chin develops a fold beneath the lower lip.

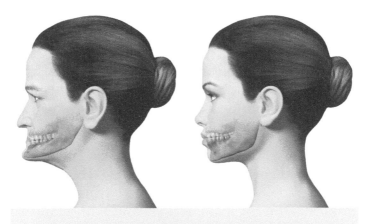

Bone resorption and its impact on the jaw and chin

Lips

There are several factors at play regarding our lips. The presence and proportions of teeth are significant. As we have seen, with ageing the maxilla (cheekbone) angles backwards, pulling the lip back and leading to deepening nasolabial folds. When the chin resorbs, the muscles in the chin exert a stronger pull, turning the chin upwards.

Lips support food intake by pushing it into the mouth cavity and holding it between our upper and lower teeth while we chew. Lips also serve to close the mouth and make it airtight to keep food and drink inside. When lips thin, not only the shape but also the function is changed, resulting in dribbling or seepage of saliva into the corner of the mouth. We need our lips to articulate sound and create facial expressions such as frowning and smiling. Lips are essential for both verbal and nonverbal communication.

Gradual tooth wear flattens our incisor edges, affecting the smile arc: the lips roll inwards and start to look thinner. Tooth loss and bone resorption lead to decreased lip projection. The cupid's bow is then less defined, and the distance between the nose and the mouth lengthens.

Finally, muscle laxity causes the corners of the mouth to drop, creating an upside-down curve associated with unhappiness. This, allied with thin, compressed lips, causes us to look older or convey a nonverbal message that we are angry or mean.

Muscles

Muscles within the face also change. Remember Mr H, whose body muscle lost its mass? Muscle loss occurs in the face, too, where the muscles lengthen and, paradoxically, increase in tone. When our face is relaxed, the increased tone of the muscle creates contractures. These contractures often occur between the eyes, increasing frown lines or compression of the lower lip and chin, further thinning the lips and contracting the chin. Muscle contractures in the lower face cause chin pebbling and, again, an upside-down mouth. The change in muscle tone also impacts the ligaments in the middle of the face, creating tissue slackness and causing cheeks to hang and the formation of jowls.

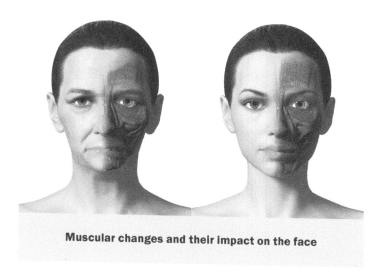

Muscular changes and their impact on the face

The muscles responsible for facial expression are mimetic muscles and the cause of dreaded smoker's lines around the lips. (Men do not have smoker's lines because they have hair follicles that support the structures beneath.)

These changes create facial characteristics which we wrongly interpret as sadness, tiredness, disapproval, contempt, meanness or anger. Many people are not even aware that their faces are behaving in this way, and it is only when people comment that they start to notice.

As if the bone and muscle change wasn't enough, we also undergo changes to our fat pads, which is the second biggest cause of facial ageing after bone.

Fat pads

There are two types of fat pads. The more significant fat pads, which provide structure to our face, are just above the bone. The other layer of fat pads is just underneath the skin. The deeper fat pads are closely packed areas of fat cells that contribute to the face's volume, shape and definition. The more superficial fat pads provide stability and contribute to the skin's general appearance. The areas where fat pads are most highly valued and seen are over the cheekbones, chin and jaw and, to a lesser extent, underneath the eyes and temples. The fat pads are thicker in the middle of the cheek and more uneven in the female than the male.

With increasing age, the fat pads change significantly: loss of subcutaneous fat (underneath the skin) decreases the support of the skin, and the loss of fat pads around the nose and upper brow causes eyelid drooping, which can start as early as the late twenties. The middle of the face is particularly affected by fat loss (and progressive muscle shortening and straightening).

The shortening of some facial muscles changes the muscle curve into a rectangular shape, expelling the fat beneath the muscle towards the superficial fat. This fat redistribution causes changes to the soft tissues seen on the outside of the face.

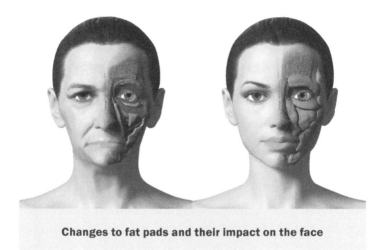

Changes to fat pads and their impact on the face

Some of the superficial fat pads undergo wasting and therefore disintegrate, shrivel or completely disappear in certain parts of the face such as under or around the eyes, mid-cheeks, nose and mouth. The changes around the eyes can be dramatic and cause tear troughs to deepen. The loss of fat pads under the eyes means that the skin now touches bone which causes darkening under the eyes and an appearance of sadness or tiredness.

Skin

Our skin is our largest organ and our first defence against several internal and external biological processes such as UV radiation, bacterial infections and chemical or mechanical stress – ageing as a result.

The skin consists of two primary layers: the dermis (inner layer) and the epidermis (outer layer). Each has a unique function.

Epidermis

The epidermis, also known as the stratum corneum, or outer layer, functions as a barrier for our body against the outside world. It faces daily onslaughts such as toxins, radiation and injury. The epidermis consists of layers of dead cells, or keratinocytes, whose sole purpose is to protect us against radiation. Coating our skin surface is a combination known as the acid mantle, which is made up of sebum, our natural skin oil and sweat. The acid mantle acts as a barrier against bacteria, viruses and other potential contaminants. Skin is said to be balanced when its pH is between around 4.5 and 5.75 (ie slightly acidic), as this allows microflora on the skin to thrive, protecting it and keeping it clean. Microflora prevent the colonisation of harmful bacteria, or pathogens, and are part of our body's defence mechanism.[30]

Skin is considered excessively alkaline when its pH is above 7. A high pH of 9 is a sign that the stratum corneum is defective. The causes of increased alkalinity are not fully understood, but it seems that it can be due to certain soaps and detergents. If the skin is too alkaline, its natural lipids (fats) are depleted, and it becomes dry and sensitive. Eczema is a sign of extreme alkalinity. Elderly people often have alkaline skin, which is consequently dry and flaky.

Skin with a pH below 4.5 is too acidic. Again, the causes of acidic skin are complex, but it mostly results from an excess of lactic acid, which occurs naturally through sweat and skin metabolic processes. Paradoxically, the proliferation of microflora also plays a role in acidifying skin. If the skin is too acidic, it becomes red, oily and pimply and will appear greasy, feel irritated and react sensitively.

Regulating and balancing our skin's pH is therefore essential and can be done in several ways: through diet or supplementation and by a correct skincare regime.

Ceramides are another important factor in our skin's condition. Ceramides are natural fatty acids that are found in high concentrations in the membrane of cells and act like the mortar in a wall, holding the cells together. Ceramides also act as a barrier, locking moisture in and preventing dryness and irritation. Without ceramides, the skin will lose fluid, resulting in diseases such as eczema, psoriasis and contact dermatitis. Ceramides protect the skin from environmental damage. Without them the skin barrier can be broken, leading to various microbial infections; if these persist, with prolonged or deeper penetration of pathogens, they can lead to compromised immunity.

Ceramides deteriorate with age, causing the skin to thin and its barrier function to weaken. Retaining the skin's proper biological function is heavily dependent on adequate nutrition in the form of lipids and the structural proteins in the form of Omega-3 and Omega-6 fatty acids, which are present in products such as oily fish, olive oil, seeds, nuts and avocados. The skin's functions can also be preserved by the use of products that lock moisture into the skin.

Dermis

The dermis contains nerves, blood vessels, connective tissue, hair follicles and fibroblasts. Fibroblasts play a key role in the health of our skin tissues as they are the source of ECM. Fibroblasts contain growth factors that make collagen and elastin and trigger various responses within our skin. For example, collagen's function is to maintain the framework of our skin, giving it strength and structure.

ECM undergoes remodelling as a result of injury, illness, poor nutrition and ageing, which produce an enzyme called matrix metalloproteinase (MMP) that breaks down collagen. It begins its dirty work around the age of twenty-eight and depletes our collagen by 1% per year. During menopause, we lose a further 30% of our collagen, which also depletes our elastin, resulting in a loss of skin elasticity. There is also a breakdown of GAG, another ingredient of ECM. GAGs link to water and fill the space between collagen and elastin fibres to give skin its plumpness. The breakdown of GAGs results in skin dryness, laxity and wrinkling. Due to ageing our skin cycle lengthens and the slower skin turnover results in dull and uneven skin.

If we do not protect our skin against UV radiation, it will suffer further tremendous damage. UV rays stimulate the production of unstable molecules such as free radicals, or ROS – remember those? Our body has a protective mechanism that tries to keep ROS below a toxic threshold. Ageing and persistent stress reach a point where the skin becomes oxidised, leading to damage at a cellular level.

The UV rays that cause ROS further break down our precious collagen, which is now poorly constructed. This causes dysfunctional skin, where the skin barrier is compromised, leading to the problems discussed earlier as well as damaged DNA. It also leads to abnormal production of melanin (freckles), pigment changes such as old age spots, and telangiectasia – weakness in blood vessels and walls that causes blue-brown discolouration of the skin. These signs are often associated with ageing and are visible in older people's hands, arms, legs and face.

Apart from the ageing caused by changes in our hormones and nutrition, our skin also suffers assault from our environment through UV radiation, toxic substances and injury, resulting in more damage that leads to lines and wrinkles.

Summary

We may not realise that our whole face changes due to the complex interplay between the facial muscles and their activity. The process is dynamic, affecting not only the bone but also the fat pads overlying the bone. Understanding why and how these changes occur is fundamental to any agelessness treatment.

10

Understanding Aesthetic Treatment

The UK beauty market is worth over £1.74 billion – and it's growing fast. Between 2008 and 2018, UK retail stores specialising in cosmetics and personal care increased their turnover from £2.7 billion to over £5.3 billion.[31] In 2020, the global aesthetic treatment market was valued at £86.2 billion, with an annual growth rate of 9.8%. Noninvasive procedures such as Botox and fillers dominate the market and account for the largest revenue share of 52.2%.[32] Contrary to the widely held belief that this growth has been caused by youngsters seeking treatment, it is older people who make up the bulk of the aesthetic market.[33]

The rapid growth in the market has been caused by numerous factors, including the rising number of trendsetters and influencers on mainstream social media who increase awareness of beauty and non-surgical treatments to optimise and improve ourself. The cosmetic and aesthetic industry has gone from a niche market to a widely available popular service, with increasing demand for a variety of treatments and a scramble among suppliers to meet that demand. The market is now so 'noisy' that it can be confusing.

The aesthetic market – messy and confusing

There is now a plethora of service offerings from multiple disciplines, including plastic surgeons, dermatologists, dentists, nurses, paramedics, beauticians and even lay people, offering treatments in diverse locations such as clinics, ambulances, mobile units, front rooms and back gardens. To stand out from this noisy crowd, service providers offer 'new' approaches, claiming 'unique' skills, methods and products, promising 'new technology', combination treatments, collaborations and so forth. In an attempt to define their services, practitioners use a variety of names, including aesthetics, cosmetics, beauty treatments, restoration, rejuvenation and anti-ageing. Prices range from exorbitant to dirt cheap and images of 'perfect' patients abound, showing 'before' and 'after' treatments supported by gushing testimonials. As in the Gold Rush, everyone wants to stake their claim and make their fortune. So-called 'training schools' pop up everywhere but they are not standardised or regulated, adding to the feeling that things are getting out of control.

I regularly support patients in dissolving treatments and repairing botched jobs and hear many hair-raising stories confirming the different standards of care, service provision and product advice from both patients and colleagues. I once overheard a woman who works in a garden centre announce that she was going on a one-day course to do Botox and fillers because it was more lucrative than her current job. A patient told me of an aesthetic clinic and 'academy' she had been to that had been set up by a woman and her two daughters with no training or medical background. The results make media headlines: scary images of botched jobs and disfigurement or people who were once beautiful turned into ridiculous caricatures.

Interestingly, and contrary to popular belief, such disasters are not always caused by 'beauticians' and lay practitioners but also by medical doctors and nurses. This can be partly attributed to poor training standards and unregulated treatment methods but also to an attitude among qualified practitioners that they can provide aesthetic treatments as a sideline for quick money and that a one-day course is good enough to provide them with enough knowledge and skills.

Let's attempt to unpack this confusing market and get to the heart of what aesthetic medicine is – or should be – about.

Common misconceptions and the meaning behind aesthetic treatment

Aesthetic treatments are now mainstream, but typical misconceptions still exist and provoke divided opinions and heated debate among service practitioners and contempt among the public. There are many assumptions: that older women who seek treatments are vain; that treatment is not for younger people, who don't need to pump up their faces with filler; that all aesthetic treatments result in 'trout pouts', 'frozen foreheads', 'surprised looks' and 'pillow cheeks' – in other words, that everyone who has such treatments looks 'abnormal'; that one millilitre of filler or Botox in the forehead will transform your wellbeing; that going to a doctor is 'safe' but letting a beautician administer treatment is 'unsafe'.

Aesthetic treatment is – or should be – about more than 'simply' body modification and superficial 'fixes' to make us look younger or more 'beautiful'. It should seek to improve our vital self and our quality of life. The focus should be on personalised, preventive optimisation rather than on standardised interventions. It should be on restoring balance both internally and externally, on returning us to homeostasis. In this sense, aesthetic medicine is a rather misleading term for what we are trying to do for our patients: we are in the business of 'gerontology', which concerns itself with successful ageing – what aesthetics broadly aims to do – or what I call agelessness.

Let's now look at how aesthetic treatment is viewed by the younger generation and the older generation.

The younger generation

Every woman has concerns about aesthetic treatment making her look like a caricature and almost all my patients ask that their treatments should be subtle, so that people don't know that they have had them. In the younger generation, beauty is an indicator of self-worth. Younger people are more likely to undergo body modifications such as tattoos, piercings and noninvasive treatments such as Botox and fillers. They are more likely to request sculpted jawlines, chins, noses and cheeks. Beyond this, they are acutely aware of the need for prevention and prefer to seek treatments sooner rather than later to prevent fine lines and wrinkles. I have not met one younger patient who wanted to look pouty and think that is a gross generalisation and misunderstanding of the younger patient to believe that they do.

Young people – especially adolescents – are immature in areas such as impulse control, risk assessment and moral reasoning and they rely on the amygdala, which is associated with primitive impulses of aggression, anger and fear.[34] They are prone to impulsiveness, risk-taking and susceptibility to peer pressure[35] and they are also more likely to share and flaunt the results of the treatments they undergo, exacerbating the trend.

The older generation

Older people, who make up the larger client base, have endured numerous blows and significant life changes and have lost confidence. Women of this generation may have had children, disease, stress, trauma and injuries. They may have had a life-changing experience such as a partner leaving them, discovering that their partner has been unfaithful, or losing a child. They are also experiencing hormonal changes to their bodies associated with the menopause. These changes affect their bodies both inwardly and outwardly and have physical, emotional and social impacts. None of my clients comes to me merely because of a few lines or wrinkles; they are experiencing discomfort which, for some of them, is painful. They realise that they have only one life and many years ahead which they want to enjoy fully. I have interviewed in excess of 500 women and have concluded that I am treating emotions, not lines. These women are concerned about 'fading' – becoming weak, dull, bland, characterless, colourless, unexciting, uninteresting, boring and lifeless. Without exception, they tell me that they are seeking treatment because they want to 'look and feel their best selves'; they don't want to look 'younger', they want to look 'better'; they want to 'look their old self again or near enough'; they 'don't want to fade'.

The older patient wants to restore, regenerate, prevent and improve but also beautify. They have started to notice facial changes and want to prevent things from getting worse. They want to maintain their features for as long as possible but also improve them where they can. (In aesthetics improvements are known as beautification and small changes as 'tweakments'.)

These women did not have the same information growing up as the younger generation have now on nutrition, the impact of harmful substances and the importance of skin protection, especially against UV rays. They often feel guilty about spending money on their faces, feeling the pressure to 'grow old gracefully'.

Case study: Jess

Jess was a thirty-three-year-old single working mother when she sought treatment for the first time. She worked for a health and beauty retailer and was an expert in make-up and skincare products. She was a vibrant, happy and energetic woman with a wicked sense of humour, but she was not comfortable with how she looked. She hated seeing herself in a mirror because she looked tired and haggard, which made her feel sad. She did not enjoy having her photo taken and was concerned that if she didn't do anything now, things would only get worse.

Jess asked for Botox to her forehead, believing that it would make her look and feel rejuvenated. To the untrained eye, this seems like a reasonable request, but it is a common mistake patients make. They request treatment in one area, completely missing all the other structures and lacking understanding of how they all interact with each other.

The Ageless Journey Map

My treatment of Jess involved a four-stage process, which I have developed to explain different categories of treatments and how the types of treatments within that journey progress towards agelessness. It is called an Ageless Journey Map.

The ageless journey can be broken down into four categories of treatment, each of which applies primarily to a specific age group.

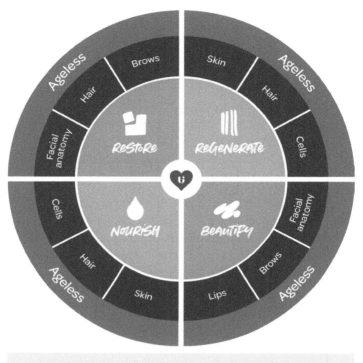

**The Ageless Journey Map: Categories of treatments
towards wellbeing and agelessness**

Beautification (tweakments)

Younger patients, as we have seen, are big on biohacking,
prevention and modification. When they seek treatments,
they focus on specific areas such as 'model' cheekbones,
'strong' jawlines, 'attractive' chins and 'seductive' lips.
They tend to seek toxin treatments to reduce large jaw
muscles (masseter muscle), to slim their faces and to
reduce fine lines and wrinkles. The majority of young

patients, like Jess, need minimal aesthetic treatment. In beautification there are usually just one or two little things that need to be tweaked.

In older patients, beautification tends to come later because they are experiencing bigger, global changes within their face. They undergo greater bone and fat pad changes, which impact most of their face and mean that more restorative work is required. New lips in an older face can look strange if done without consideration for the other anatomical changes. Just doing a lip filler when there are underlying structural issues is not the answer. The aim should be to restore the harmony of the features.

Regeneration

This category is focused on cellular improvement. The commonest treatments include skin remodelling, such as peels, needling, injectable platelets (PRP/IPRF), Profhilo, meso, laser, cosmeceutical skincare and others – the list of treatments is extensive. The aim is to prevent further degradation and revive collagen and elastin.

In certain cases, starting with regeneration results in better overall outcomes for patients, including increased patient satisfaction. By preventing further deterioration of collagen and elastin, it is possible to age less.

Regenerative treatments work on a cellular level and can reverse cell decay. They may employ genetic testing for nutrition, hair loss and telomeres, as well as blood tests. DNA tests are available to measure the age of cells, predict future illness, inflammation, chronic disease, toxicity and cellular damage. DNA tests can also advise which supplements and diets you should consider for your patients, which leads nicely into precision patient nutrition and management. It is all about tailored medicine and countering one-size-fits-all practice.

Restoration

The patients over forty-five are the ones who tend to need all four categories of treatment as they start to notice the considerable changes caused by menopause, illness, injury, childbearing, nutrition and their genetics. At this stage, the bone and fat pads in the face are already significantly resorbed and steadily deteriorating, leading to a loss of contours, mainly around the eyes, midface, jawline and chin.

Restoration means to return something to its former state. Whereas regeneration focuses on the more superficial structures to repair collagen and elastin in the skin, restoration aims to fix the deeper structures. The treatment requires injecting fillers into the deep fat pads and bone. If the damage to the skin is severe, it makes sense to start on the outside and move inwards. Only after restoring skin and bone can we proceed to beautification – putting the icing on the cake.

Nourishment

Nourishment aims to provide the sustenance which is necessary for growth and health, preventing injury and illness at a cellular level. We achieve this through a precision treatment plan of transformative and restorative skincare, nutraceutical infusions, hormone replacement and supplementation, beginning with blood and hormone testing, including DNA. Nourishment should be for life to prevent all the age-related injury and insults we have discussed in the previous chapters.

Jess required a combined approach of restoration and beautification and then nourishment to provide her with the best outcomes. She is now forty and looking better than she did when she was younger.

Summary

Ageing is unavoidable: our cells and bones are programmed to change. It is a multifactorial process, with many internal as well as external causes. The approach to agelessness is complex; unfortunately, one method will not solve all the problems – a common misconception among patients. Every patient is unique and has different genetics, health, exposure to toxins and general wellbeing, as well as a different age, and there is always hope.

11

Everything You Need To Know About Botox And Filler

When I look at Georgina and Jess following their treatments (see Chapters 9 and 10), the thing that strikes me first is the glint in their eyes, followed by the newfound confidence they ooze. They seem to get better with age, not worse. It is no wonder that cosmetic treatments are increasing in popularity and improving confidence and self-esteem. Trends in aesthetic medicine are continuously changing, but some treatments remain popular. The most popular treatments are Botox and filler. In this chapter I explain why, as well as discussing the benefits and limitations of these two types of treatment.

Botox – the 'wonder' drug

Botox is one of the most popular aesthetic treatments, with over 7.5 billion treatments performed each year worldwide, and its use is increasing annually by 7.5%.[36]

'Botox' is an abbreviation of botulinum toxin, which is a neurotoxin – one of the most poisonous substances on the planet. There are seven types of neurotoxins, which are present in plants, soil, water and the intestinal tract of animals. Only botulinum toxin A (BoNT/A) and B (BoNT/B) – which are produced by the bacterium *Clostridium botulinum* – are used to treat various medical disorders. BoNT/A has been isolated and purified into the product commonly referred to as Botox today. Botox is, however, a brand name, and several others exist but are less known, including Dysport, Xeomin, Neurobloc, Azzalure and Bocouture. To avoid confusion I will use the term Botox in the rest of this chapter. Botox is a medical product that is only available on prescription and must not be shared with anyone else. Advertising Botox is not allowed, though practitioners usually get around the law by promoting 'muscle relaxation'.

The idea of injecting a 'poison' into our bodies to improve our appearance and wellbeing seems paradoxical – and many people cannot fathom why anyone would consider doing so – but Botox is one of the reasons I started in aesthetics. The difference I saw in women's confidence following Botox treatment drew me to aesthetic medicine. I was excited to discover that there was something we could do that was so different from traditional medicine but so life-changing, and I wanted to know more.

How Botox works

Neurotoxins are destructive to nerve tissue and cause movement disorders and paralysis. The effectiveness of botulinum toxin was discovered in the 1970s, when it was used to treat strabismus (the condition of being cross-eyed). The toxin was found to relax the muscles pulling the eyes inwards by causing muscle paralysis. It was also discovered that the effect does not last long because the body has the unique ability to sprout new nerve terminals in two to three months.

BoNT/A injections are performed millions of times a year around the world.[37] Botox is currently one of the most versatile pharmaceuticals for the treatment of human diseases in ophthalmology, neurology and dermatology and has also become integrated into popular culture as a cosmetic enhancement tool for the ageing population.

Botox is commonly used in aesthetics to relax muscles in the face that close the eye and create hooded skin, causing what are known as frown lines and crow's feet. Botox can also be used to improve facial harmony, treating features such as flared nasal turbinates (large nose entrances), pebble chins and bunny lines (lines across the nose). It can be injected into the masseter muscles to prevent teeth grinding, which results in squaring of the face.

We have facial vectors that determine the position of one point in the face in relation to another. For instance, vector muscles in the forehead work with the upper muscles pulling up and the lower muscles pulling down. Understanding this is essential to the correct use of Botox, which causes the muscles to interact with each other. Because most patients do not know about vectors, they usually request treatment in only one area, but this is rarely ideal because it neglects other areas that might generate a much better outcome.

The clinician should assess a patient's anatomy in three dimensions, observing their facial features both in relaxation and in movement, such as frowning, smiling and surprise. The reaction of the muscles during these movements will indicate the areas requiring treatment. Facial structure should also be taken into consideration. Patients are not necessarily aware that their nose tip is dipping, that their chin is blunted and turning up, or that their eyelids are resting on their lashes. It is therefore up to the clinician to determine the areas of treatment based on the patient's unique features.

Injecting Botox

Before injecting Botox, you should undergo a full medical assessment regarding disease, drugs and allergies. The consultation must also cover the risks, expectations and possible side effects before you sign a consent form. Your face must then be cleaned with an antibacterial medical product to prevent any risk of infection. Sterile dressing packs should be used and discarded according to infection protocol.

Larger and thicker muscles will usually receive a larger dose than smaller, fine muscles. Treatment requires in-depth knowledge of each muscle – especially where it begins and ends – so that the toxin does not stray into adjacent muscles, causing unwanted complications such as a droopy eye or smile or 'Spock's eyebrow', or the patient resembling an 'angry bird'.

The effect of Botox injections is gradual and usually reaches a peak in two to three weeks, though some patients report a noticeable response within a few days or even hours. The effect lasts around three to four months, which means repeated treatment is required. In some patients the effect wears off after two months because of their high metabolism.

Safety and efficacy

The paradox that Botox is a highly toxic substance that we inject into our face needs to be considered. During my master's training in aesthetic medicine, I researched and critically analysed multiple large studies carried out over the period of ten years on the safety and efficacy of Botox.

Botox has been processed and purified (it was first purified way back in the 1920s and has continued to be improved upon ever since) and is injected in small quantities. Multiple studies show that Botox has a safety profile comparable to a placebo and is highly effective across a broad spectrum of indications. It has an excellent tolerability profile and does not cause persistent changes or long-term adverse effects (see below). Idiosyncratic reactions do occur but are uncommon. In treating over 9,000 patients, I have had only three with pronounced – and different – adverse reactions: dry eyes, hair loss and anxiety. In general, my patients feel less depressed, more excited, happier and more confident after treatment.

Side effects

Side effects can occur in some patients. These are varied, but the most common ones are:

- Pain or swelling at the injection site

- Bruising

- Slight lumps (eg on the forehead) initially but these usually settle quickly, generally within half an hour

- Headaches, especially on the first treatment

- Slight flu symptoms on the first treatment, which don't usually last longer than twenty-four hours

- Allergic reactions are infrequent.

Botox aftercare

Since Botox is a precision injection, anything that can cause infection or spreading of the product into unwanted muscles should be avoided. In particular, you should observe the following guidelines:

- Don't touch the treated area.

- Don't do strenuous exercise.

- Don't lie down for at least four hours.

- Wash your face gently the evening after treatment.

- Avoid drinking alcohol, which can thin the blood and increase the spread of toxins or worsen bruising.

Botox is mainly used in the upper face and chin. For bone and fat pad loss, the only effective treatment is fillers.

Filler

Fillers are popular due to their diversity and versatility. There are essentially two types of filler: temporary fillers consist of a synthetic hyaluronic acid, a sugar compound usually found within the skin and connective tissue; long-lasting fillers consist of calcium hydroxylapatite, a substance primarily found in bone. It is thicker than hyaluronic acid and, instead of plumping the skin, it stimulates collagen production. Its effect is not as immediate as in hyaluronic acid, making it a less popular treatment. It can also only be used in certain areas, such as the cheeks, chin and jawline. Because filler mimics natural hyaluronic acid, it follows the skin repair cycle, degrading and then replenishing itself. It lasts for around six to twelve months – longer in some cases.

Filler is used to repair injuries (eg facial changes after facial fractures), correct 'deformities' (eg an underdeveloped chin), improve scars and replace lost volume. Fillers can project (chin, lips, cheeks), sculpt (jawlines, eye sockets, temples) or fill out (vaginal walls and facial features). Filler can also be used within the labia majora of the vagina to counteract the loss of moistness caused by menopause.

The purpose of fillers is to rejuvenate the face by restoring volume and contours eroded by bone resorption. When filler is injected deeply, it restores and supports the skeletal foundation and facial structure, also improving the surrounding skin. As a result, different strengths and consistencies exist for specific outcomes. Areas where a lot of tissue or a large area of (or heavy) skin is involved, such as temples, cheeks, jawline and chin, will require a more robust filler. Thinner or more delicate skin, such as under the eyes or in the lip, will need a less intense filler.

Injecting filler

Before injecting your face, the clinician should determine your needs and concerns. You should also be advised about the risks and possible side effects (see below). You may feel anxious or even be unable to tolerate this type of treatment. Your face must then be cleaned with an antibacterial medical solution to reduce the risk of infection. Photographs are a requirement for insurance purposes but also to compare the before and after attributes.

Before treatment commences, your face should be assessed in its three dimensions both in movement and at rest, considering the five areas where change occurs: bone, fat pads, muscle, superficial fat pads and skin. The treatment areas should be clearly marked before treatment starts. Identifying and marking the danger zones and superficial arteries is paramount in reducing risk.

Filler injections need to be in the proper planes using the correct filler and delivery mechanism such as a needle or cannula. Injections must be slow and measured, taking care to minimise injury and adverse reactions. If you experience severe pain, the clinician should stop injecting and investigate the cause. There are several reasons for pain, including injecting into an artery or bone, hitting a nerve, using inappropriate filler or having an inadequate injection technique.

When treating patients with filler, 'less is more' is the best approach. More can always be added. Injecting filler is like pouring custard onto pebbles. The filler initially lies on top of the skin tissue before integrating with it and drawing moisture from it. Because filler attracts fluid, too much can cause bloating, which usually occurs in lips and cheeks and under the eyes. Too much filler can also distort the anatomy of the bone and fat pads. A classic example is where filler rides so high on the cheek that it pushes the cheeks into the eyes, making the eyes look smaller and the smile abnormal. Another is where too much lip filler is used in the wrong planes and outside the specific lip borders or in too many quantities resulting in a 'duck' look or 'trout pout'.

Safety and efficacy

Dermal filler has now become mainstream and is one of the most performed procedures. The use of filler has soared from 1.8 million procedures in 2010 to 2.6 million in 2016 and is still gaining momentum.[38] The Federal Drug Agency, whose protocols are followed in the UK, has approved various filler materials, each with a distinct composition, injection profile and duration of effect; in clinical trials, these were shown to cause few adverse reactions. However, the widespread use of fillers by a variety of practitioners and the plethora of brands worldwide, coupled with an unreliable data collection method, make it difficult to determine the incidence of complications accurately. There is no database in the UK for reporting adverse events and difficulties, for example.

To ensure that you get the best possible treatment, here are the questions to ask:

- Has the provider had rigorous scientific training, as is expected of nurses, doctors, paramedics, pharmacists and other medical professionals, and is there a team with a high standard of training and support?

- Are their products biodegradable, compatible with the tissues and of nonanimal origin?

- Do the products integrate with the skin tissues for the most natural outcome?

- Is the filler dissolvable? Fillers need to be dissolved in case they occlude the blood flow to another structure, which is one of the risks to consider before you give consent (see below). Some long-lasting fillers are not dissolvable and some new products on the market have no safety history and might therefore not be fully dissolvable.

- Do the products offer long-lasting results?

After treatment, the face is cleaned again and 'sculpted', ensuring that the filler is in the correct planes and evenly distributed, primarily over the lips and cheeks.

Filler treatments have immediate effects, which usually further improve after a few days. The patient should consume plenty of fluid. Most patients can go straight back to work after treatment, but there is a risk of swelling and bruising, especially in the lips.

Side effects

However much care is taken in identifying areas where veins are located and in the injecting itself, bruising and swelling are common. The injection site can feel bruised for a few days, and sometimes a tingling sensation remains, possibly caused by an injured nerve. (This isn't typical and doesn't last long.) Other possible side effects are:

- A temporary redness and some lumps while the filler settles through the tissue.

- Some discolouration, especially when using a topical anaesthetic. If discolouration persists and is accompanied by pain (particularly if you press the area for five seconds and the colour does not return within two seconds), you must ask for a review sooner rather than later.

- Lumps, which need attention if they persist but are easy to rectify by massage. Lumps caused by superficial filler placement might require draining with a needle.

- Infections, which can occur if your clinician did not clean your face adequately before a procedure or you touched your face too soon after the procedure.

- Nodules, which can occur months or years down the line, sometimes as a side effect of another treatment as your body's defence mechanism recognises the filler as foreign, causing inflammation. Analgesia and antibiotics generally resolve the problem.

- Filler migration, especially to active parts of the face, such as the mouth and eyes.

- Distortion and puffiness around the cheeks and eyes, caused by repeated filler treatment. Your face can also become puffy due to hormonal changes or the onset of your period, which can exacerbate the effect of the filler, especially in the lips or under the eyes. This should, however, settle within a few days.

Filler aftercare is usually given by clinicians, but is essentially the same as for Botox.

Complications

Most complications resulting from filler treatment are relatively minor and easy to resolve. A more severe complication can occur, known as vascular or venous occlusion, which in rare cases can cause:

- Skin necrosis (gangrene)

- Blindness

- Stroke

To minimise the risk of such outcomes, your practitioner must have a thorough understanding of the anatomy of the face, knowledge of the dangerous injection sites and mastery of injection techniques. Studying anatomy books alone is insufficient preparation for the safe use of filler.

Summary

Despite ever-changing trends in aesthetic medicine, Botox and filler remain among the most popular treatments. Each has benefits and potential side effects which your clinician must be fully cognisant of and explain fully to you before any treatment is undertaken.

12

Ageless Skin

For women especially, glowing, healthy skin is the epitome of physical attractiveness and upward mobility. Each ancient society – in India, Africa and Europe – had their skincare passed down through generations. The ancient Egyptians believed that the skin should be cleansed, treated and moisturised, using sea salt to remove impurities, milk and honey to hydrate, and almond and moringa oil to soften the skin and reduce wrinkles. Most of us have learned about skincare from our mothers, who learned from their mothers and so on.

Skincare remains a primary part of the wellbeing industry in the twenty-first century, and its essential 'message' remains the same: look after your skin and it will look after you as it is a window to your vitality. To a certain extent, this is true: a well-designed skincare regime can yield results comparable to those of invasive procedures, so I aim to put skincare first in everything I do; but, as in any overcrowded market, there is such a bewildering variety of skincare products it is easy to get it wrong when choosing what works for you.

The ten common mistakes when choosing skincare products

1. Making a decision based on price: believing that paying £400 for a pot of moisturiser made by a well-known company guarantees good results or, conversely, choosing a cheap product because it is better than nothing.

2. Being seduced by the packaging and adverts: going for the best-looking packaging or the products that are most widely advertised.

3. Being taken in by fashionable buzzwords (being a 'skintellectual'): thinking that if the blurb mentions hyaluronic acid, GAGs, retinol, plumping, etc the product must be good.

4. Believing that the more steps in the skincare regime, the better the outcome: using double cleansing or two different products, involving up to ten steps.

5. Choosing brands with 'integrity' claims.

6. Buying products with celebrity endorsements: forgetting that the celebrities are paid for this and get the product for free; they don't necessarily use it and it doesn't necessarily work.

7. Choosing skincare aimed at neglected demographics, with names such as 'black girl' or 'Korean skincare'.

8. Trusting that what works for someone else will work for you: eg 'My mother had great skin and she only ever used X.'

9. Believing that the answer to everything is to moisturise, when in fact by over-moisturising you shut your own skin's moisturising cycle (a phenomenon known as reverse engineering).

10. Thinking that plain water and wipes are enough.

It is challenging to make an informed decision with so much choice of products and so many 'expert' opinions out there. Who do you trust and where do you start?

The correct skincare for you must contain the right active ingredients, which act in a particular order that will transform your cells' function. Older skin often needs to be regenerated, whereas younger skin needs to be protected so that damage is prevented.

Our skin has an acid mantle that protects it from daily onslaughts, including those by most topical skincare treatments. Most skincare products and cosmetics stay on the surface due to the acid mantle. To modify cells, products need to penetrate to the deeper layers, where healing and repair can occur. Such products are known as cosmeceuticals.

Cosmeceuticals

The term cosmeceutical is yet another hybrid word: a combination of 'cosmetics' and 'pharmaceutical'. Cosmeceuticals have active ingredients that perform a biological action in the skin and designed delivery systems that allow them to reach deeper layers within the skin. Total chemical purity means that a product contains a single substance, without any other element tarnishing its standalone existence. Pharmaceutical products are highly regulated, and products are required to be 99% chemically pure. Ingredients within cosmeceutical products must be 70% pure and have a high quality of other elements within the formulation ingredients.

Cosmetics are different to cosmeceuticals. A typical cosmetic product will contain anything from fifteen to fifty ingredients and over 3,000 chemicals used to formulate the huge range of fragrances used in consumer products worldwide. Considering the average woman uses between nine and fifteen personal care products per day, researchers have estimated that, when combined with the addition of perfumes, women place around 515 individual chemicals on their skin each day through cosmetic use.[39] In our pursuit of beauty, it is wise to remember that cosmetics can be complex combinations of chemicals. As a cosmetic product can only be applied to the outer surface of the skin it cannot directly treat a specific disease, whereas the main purpose of cosmeceuticals is to restore, correct or modify the physiological functions through pharmacological action.

Case study: Bev

Bev worked in a busy corporate environment and attended regular meetings at a regional level. With the advent of the Covid-19 pandemic, her meetings went online and, seeing herself on camera, she noticed her skin more than ever. Bev is in her late fifties and her skin was showing the usual signs of ageing. It was dull, lined and pigmented with slow skin turnover. Its texture and colouring were uneven. Bev and her skin both looked tired, which made her feel old and dull. She wanted something that would renew her skin – and her confidence.

Interpreting Bev's skin the pigmentation is clearly visible, including fine lines and wrinkles (an indication of lack of collagen) and a general dullness with the uneven skin texture and tone we usually see in ageing. Bev would need a systematic approach to restore structure, remove pigmentation and even out texture. I call this approach the 5C Skincare Programme.

The 5C Skincare Programme

The aims of the 5C Skincare Programme are to clean the skin of all bacteria and harmful substances or old oil and debris; change its pH so that products can penetrate better or stabilise the skin; increase cell turnover (shift old cells and move young cells up quicker); clear skin from conditions such as acne, pigmentation and rosacea; and finally improve its condition, ie its texture, elasticity and collagen, by stimulating the production of fibroblasts and then protect it from the sun to prevent renewed damage.

Clean

Clean skin is healthy skin. Our skin is the largest organ of our body, so keeping it in top condition should be a priority throughout life. A healthy skincare programme begins with a cleansing regime designed for your specific needs and skin type. Good cleansers will work with your skin and not strip it of its natural oils. The purpose of a cleanser is to remove dirt, sebum (excess oil), microorganisms and exfoliated corneum cells in an emulsified form, which it should do without irritating, damaging or disrupting the skin and its acid mantle. Water alone removes about 65% of oil and dirt but is less effective at removing oils left by cosmetics and environmental damage.

Exfoliators work chemically and mechanically to help clear clogged pores that cause dull, dry, uneven skin. They thoroughly cleanse skin to reveal a soft, smooth and radiant complexion.

If you have dry or sensitive skin, use a specifically formulated gentle cleanser to clean and soothe. Gentle cleansers contain ingredients such as apricot kernel oil and glycerine, which act as emollients to smooth and hydrate the skin.

Change pH

As we have seen, our skin surface wears a coat known as the acid mantle, which combines sebum, natural skin oil and sweat and acts as a barrier against bacteria, viruses and other potential contaminants that might penetrate our skin. The skin's ideal acidity is a pH of between 4.5 and 5.75. If the skin is too acidic (low pH), it becomes red, oily and pimply; when it is too alkaline (high pH), it becomes dry and sensitive.

Regulating and balancing your skin's pH is essential. Most soaps have a pH level between 9 and 10, so they are not good for alkaline skin as your sebaceous glands overproduce to compensate and clog your pores or create breakouts. Soaps can also erode your skin's structure. Cleansers and toners aim to change the pH of the skin so that the active ingredients in treatments can penetrate the skin and directly impact the cells.

Toners are one of the most neglected steps in skincare regimes as they are seen as just another 'money-making extra'. However, the actual function of toners is to restore the skin's natural pH. Toners should be applied when skin is wet to allow for easier penetration. They then lock in moisture and offer extra protection. Many toners are infused with antioxidants to protect your skin against free radicals. The use of toners results in visibly smoother skin and makes it harder for debris to penetrate.

Cells – increase and improve cell turnover

The aim of this stage of the 5C process is to get rid of dead cells that are sitting on the surface of your skin (corneocytes) and increase and improve epidermal turnover. Increased cell turnover is a game-changer, with results that parallel Botox and filler injections. Removing dead skin means reducing skin thickness, eliminating dullness and improving fine lines and wrinkles, reflecting light and making the skin brighter and more luminous.

Eliminating dead skin needs to be done at a chemical level by using acids to peel off the outer layer. When old dead skin is removed new skin needs to move to the surface – epidermal turnover and increased collagen build-up. It also improves even distribution of melanin (pigment), further improving skin discolouration caused by pigment. Acids must penetrate the skin, and to do that, they need to have a low pH. The lower the acid number the deeper the acid penetrates. Chemical peels are classified according to their depth of penetration of the skin into superficial to medium depth. The depth of penetration is determined by the concentration, pH and type of peeling agent used.[40]

Clear – improve damage, injury and disease

This step involves the use of active ingredients and is essential in any skincare regime. Active ingredients aim to clear skin of problems such as acne, pigmentation, rosacea and ageing. Some functions do overlap but each active ingredient has a primary function, and the treatment product will be different depending on the complaint.

The principal active ingredients are antioxidants, hydroquinone and retinoid.

Antioxidants (vitamin C)

Remember free radicals, which cause damage to our DNA? They are caused by pollutants, the environment, metabolic processes and UV radiation, among other things. Take skin pigmentation for example. When our skin (to be precise, our melanocyte) detects the sun's rays, it releases melanin to protect it (so the darker our skin, the better it is protected from the sun). During ageing the production of melanin in our skin becomes uneven and irregular and we tend to develop sunspots and freckles.

Antioxidants, which contain vitamin C, inhibit the production of melanin, thereby reducing unwanted pigmentation. They also happen to promote collagen production, restoring the skin's suppleness, and regenerate vitamin E. Vitamin E's primary role is to moisturise and smooth the skin but it is also an antioxidant.

To improve its effectiveness, you can supplement with vitamin C orally or intravenously while applying treatments onto the skin. Other products rich in antioxidants are berries and green tea.

Hydroquinone

Antioxidants are good for pigmentation and evening out skin colour, especially in younger skin. The Rolls Royce of pigment treatments is hydroquinone, which is mildly acidic and therefore able to reach much deeper into the skin and stop the melanocyte producing melanin, greatly reducing skin discolouration and restoring skin to an even colour all over.

Retinoid (vitamin A)

The showstopper and the workhorse in every skin-care regime is good old vitamin A – aka retinoid. Retinoid goes by various names depending on the way it is compounded; these include retinaldehyde, retinoic acid and tretinoin. I favour tretinoin, which comes in different strengths and for which you will require a prescription.

Tretinoin's most important function by far is its capacity to regenerate collagen. In Chapter 9 we discussed MMP – those little enzymes that break down the production of ECM from around the age of twenty-eight. Tretinoin acts on MMP by forcing it to stay open and continue producing collagen and elastin. The result is tightening skin (thanks to elastin), reduction of fine lines and wrinkles (thanks to collagen) and increased cell turnover. Like acids, it removes old skin and allows new skin to reach the surface, reducing dullness and revealing a more luminescent complexion. The thicker new skin at the surface further contributes to reducing superficial veins caused by sun damage and improves blood circulation, contributing to the image of youth and wellbeing. Tretinoin is also used in acne manage-ment as it controls oil production, which reduces pores, and to treat carbuncles, acne and rosacea.

In short, vitamin A derivatives are one of the best anti-ageing treatments on the market.

Condition

The aim of condition is to further support and improve the skin through various other modalities. When we learn about skincare, usually from our mothers or friends, they tell us, 'moisturise, moisturise, moisturise'; we are led to believe that it is one of the most important parts of a skincare regime. However, some dermatologists propose that, on the contrary, traditional moisturisers may worsen our skins and should be avoided.[41] Instead, they suggest that we should hydrate our skin using humectants, substances that lock water within the skin and prevent water loss through evaporation.

Moisturisers

Moisturisers are the most common skincare product, which almost every person in the world is familiar with and millions use prolifically to 'condition' their skin. Some moisturisers can do your skin more harm than good. The endodermis (deeper layer) is where all the hormonal balancing and messaging takes place. It messages the exodermis (outer layer) to see if it requires moisture. If we continuously apply gooey moisturisers, our exodermis signals to the dermis that it does not need moisturising, so the endodermis withholds moisture and the skin continues to feel dry, resulting in us applying more moisturiser, further perpetuating the problem.

Some moisturisers are occlusive, so the skin isn't able to breathe. The moisturiser sticks to the corneocytes on the surface, making the skin appear thick and dull and creating the total opposite of what you want to achieve.

Good moisturising agents are ceramides, nicotinamide, pantothenic acid and dexpanthenol. These penetrate the stratum corneum easily, enhancing the skin's barrier function. As we have seen, ceramides are long fatty acid chains that promote cellular function but, more importantly, create a barrier that locks moisture in the skin and prevents dryness and irritation. Nicotinamide is an essential vitamin (B3) that influences many skin processes and is also a potent antioxidant to enhance the barrier function of the skin and stimulate the production of ceramides. Both vitamin B3 and ceramides regulate cell regeneration, improve the barrier and protect against water loss. They are also anti-ageing agents, reducing fine lines and wrinkles and improving skin elasticity and colour. Pantothenic acid (B5) is a water-soluble vitamin from the B group of vitamins that helps to restore the skin's natural hydration balance while repairing damaged skin tissue. It is for all skin types, but especially for dry and dehydrated skin. Dexpanthenol acts like a moisturiser, improving stratum corneum hydration, reducing water loss through the skin and maintaining skin softness and elasticity.

Sunscreen

It is important to remember that sunburn is not actually caused by heat from the sun, but rather the radiation that the sun produces. The sun releases UV radiation in two different wavelengths – UVA and UVB – and both are harmful in different ways.

UVA is a longer wavelength, which penetrates deep into the skin and causes cellular damage. UVA exposure often leads to premature ageing, skin discolouration and wrinkles. UVB has a shorter wavelength and damages the surface of the skin. The damage from UVB is more severe, as it can cause freckles, moles, sunburn and cancer. It is imperative that the new skin which we have achieved by using the active ingredients is now protected from further UV damage.

Two major strategies exist to avoid sun damage, which include a combination of protective clothing and appropriate sunscreen. UV protection requires either absorbing or scattering photons.[42] Sunscreen containing zinc oxide or titanium dioxide will both absorb and scatter UV photons. Unlike other compounds used in sunscreens, which may absorb only a part of the UV radiation, titanium dioxide is extremely efficient at protecting against all aspects of UV light that can affect skin.

I applied the 5C process to Bev and she had a spectacular outcome. It was visible not only on her skin, but also in her smile and her eyes. Her skin was now luminescent, with increased collagen. The age spots caused by hyperpigmentation were gone, and the texture and colour were flawless. Fine lines and wrinkles had significantly improved, and she had a newfound glow. The skincare treatment resulted in Bev looking years younger with increased confidence. She is now becoming ageless.

Bev before and after, enjoying her newfound glow

Summary

Collagen and elastin are where the focus on skincare lies. Apart from skincare to condition the skin, we rely on other modalities to continue to improve the production of collagen and elastin. Some we have already covered, such as oral supplementation, hormone replacement therapies, adequate nutrition in its various forms from diet to intravenous treatments and skincare; other skincare regimes will be discussed in the following chapters – they all fall under conditioning.

13

The 7S Process
For Agelessness

In the last chapter we looked at the 5C Skincare Programme, a skincare regime that will repair, rejuvenate, revitalise and restore your skin. As we have seen, looking and feeling your best is about more than just taking care of your skin. My experience of treating patients over the last thirty years has resulted in a holistic, total-body programme I have called the 7S Process for Agelessness: Story, Structure, Strategy, Shape, Supplement, Skin, Sustain.

In the rest of this chapter I will use Jess's and Georgina's stories to illustrate how the process works. We met Georgina in Chapter 9 and Jess in Chapter 10. I would first like to emphasise that I will not treat patients if they do not need it, and that I do not take on patients if I believe that I will never be able to satisfy their needs. This is often due to a phenomenon known as body dysmorphia.

Body dysmorphia

Body dysmorphia is a mental disorder characterised by a preoccupation with a particular aspect of one's appearance. An individual will frequently touch the area of concern, looking at it from all angles. They seek constant confirmation that the area is terrible, or reassurance that it is not as bad as someone else's. This preoccupation can result in severe distress and have a social and emotional impact. When a new patient walks through my door and is obviously distressed by an area of their face, alarm bells go off. I have refused to treat patients who have body dysmorphia as I firmly believe that no matter what I do, they will never be happy. Instead, I send them back to their GP, suggesting a mental health referral.

In both Jess's and Georgina's case, I was satisfied that they were not suffering from body dysmorphia.

Jess

Jess had come to me requesting Botox for her forehead because she felt that her lines made her look old. Like many of my patients, she had an idea of what she needed to feel happier. She had researched local clinics, treatment procedures and facial makeover programmes.

We all tend to examine ourselves one-dimensionally and often only focus on one particular area. Most people don't know about the five layers that need addressing or appreciate the importance of hormones or nutrition. My patients often believe that treating a specific area will solve all their problems and tend to be prescriptive of their treatments, unconsciously unaware that they might need a combined approach to give them better results.

Story

The aim of the first consultation is to get to know you (the patient), find out all the reasons you are ageing and determine where you are situated in Maslow's Hierarchy of Needs. Knowing this detail supports decision making in choosing the relevant ageless pathway towards wellbeing and improved appearance. It is also important to know about any relevant medical illnesses, injuries, allergies and medication you may be taking which can be contraindicated in treatments or increase risk of bleeding and bruising. I am constantly looking for nonverbal clues to your condition, as these often reveal more than words. I also use the opportunity to tell you my story, experience and expertise, and what you can expect from treatment. I try to establish a relationship of trust and mutual understanding so that you can feel confident in my treatment.

Every one of us has a story based on our journey through life. Along the route, something happens that triggers us to seek treatment. Jess was no different. To add to the pressures of being a single working mum she had recently had to deal with the loss of both her parents and did not have siblings. She was suffering with increased anxiety and had become self-conscious that she was looking more haggard, which made her feel insecure about herself.

Structure

The next step is to analyse your facial anatomy and structural changes in all three dimensions, including animation and rest. Understanding the anatomical changes that have taken place helps determine the treatment strategy. This is known as an anatomological approach, which means a logical approach to anatomy. The structural assessment is from top to bottom, left to right, and divides the face into three areas: forehead, midface and lower face.

In Jess's case, she had a relatively large forehead and small lower face. Her forehead was lined and she had hooding on the outer corners of her eyes, creating a 'sad' droop. Her temples were more hollowed, exacerbating the droop around the sides of her eyes. The fat pad losses in her midface had deepened her tear troughs, emphasising the 'sad' look. Her nose was slightly misaligned and was one of the things that bothered her most. There was a disconnect between her chin and her jawline, the chin seeming isolated from the rest of her face. Jess's lips were well proportioned, but she wanted them to be more prominent.

Lastly, Jess's skin was oily and, she told me, burned easily if unprotected. Her skin colour and texture were uneven, with pigmentation on her forehead, cheeks and mouth and, particularly around her mouth and chin, it felt rough to touch.

Strategy

I explained to Jess what was happening on the inside and outside of her face, and together we planned her treatment strategy. We would use Botox to reduce the lines and wrinkles on her forehead and pull her eyebrows up and apart. We would use filler for her cheeks, tear troughs, lips and lower face in all the areas depicted in yellow in the following image where there are losses. Finally, we would use skin peels to remove the outer dead layer of her skin (see Chapter 14), followed by transformative skincare to stimulate collagen production, increase skin turnover and even out her skin colour and texture.

Shape

It is now time to put the treatment plan into practice by actively restoring and improving the areas that have undergone an anatomical change. The areas are marked out with a pencil and then injected and sculpted accordingly.

Supplement

Most patients who seek aesthetic treatment are changing at a cellular level, as we have been discussing throughout the book. Menopausal women undergo significant facial bone and tissue remodelling. Treating the outside with Botox and fillers will help, but addressing the causes of the change will have far more significant outcomes in the long run.

Accurate testing of hormones, nutrition and blood can further enhance patient outcomes, especially their wellbeing, and prevent ongoing deterioration. For many women this is still an area of contention, and they are generally less keen to invest their hard-earned money in supplementing than in treating their skin.

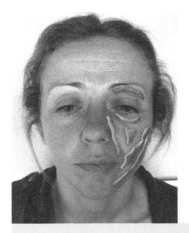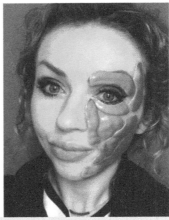

Jess restored. The image indicates the areas where filler was inserted to restore the lost fat pads but also shows the difference Botox has made to her forehead and eyes and the effect of the skin treatments in creating luminescence.

Skin

As we saw in the previous chapter, skin is the most important aspect of all to treat but often the most neglected. Correct skin treatment delivers results that equal and, in many cases, better invasive treatments.

Often skin treatment is the first port of call before shaping the face; this is because of loss of collagen and elastin. The aim is always to improve skin turnover, boost collagen and elastin production, and remove unsightly age spots, scars and uneven skin texture, creating a fresh, clear canvas before toxins and fillers are injected. It often reduces the amounts needed and helps achieve longer-lasting results.

By improving Jess's skin, I gave it a new luminosity and freshness. Her make-up also went on better.

Sustain

For many people, the cost of aesthetic treatment is prohibitive. Maintaining excellent outcomes sometimes means injecting more filler and Botox, involving additional cost and often producing diminishing results. There comes a time where we reach saturation point, and it is best to look at other means to continue supporting maximum outcomes in the form of combination treatments and supplementation. We will be looking at these in the final chapter.

First, let's see how the 7S Process for Agelessness was applied in Georgina's case.

Georgina

The first time Georgina set foot in my clinic, I knew there was much more going on than just lines and wrinkles. Georgina looked life-tired. She had obviously been kicked in the teeth one too many times;

it showed in her whole demeanour. I sat Georgina down, looking for nonverbal clues while listening to her story.

Story

Sure enough, before long there were tears. She had been involved in a severe car accident many years before, and this had affected one side of her face, as well as her right hand and knee. She has been diagnosed with fibromyalgia, which meant that she had days of agony in every fibre of her body, along with tiredness and brain fog. She had grown children but a broken relationship, and her new partner drank excessively. She was not working but was a carer for her elderly mother and disabled sister.

Georgina was deeply unhappy, and tired of feeling tired. She could not remember the last time she felt well, and the combination of physical, social and emotional stress was playing havoc with her wellbeing. Georgina further explained that she had spent a lot of money on her face with many highly qualified plastic surgeons and aesthetic practitioners, but nothing seemed to help. After taking Georgina's history, I was reassured that she did not have body dysmorphia and placed her on tier two of Maslow's Hierarchy of Needs, which meant that we had a long way to go to self-actualisation. After Georgina had poured her heart out, it was time to get to work.

I sat Georgina in front of a mirror. I wanted her to show me what she felt she needed and what would make her happy. Typically, she pulled, prodded and shaped everything in her face, getting more unhappy by the minute, and said she thought she would look better if she just had a bit of treatment around her cheeks.

Structure

I explained the various layers to Georgina using an anatomical model and then related it to her face. I explained the changes and treatments required in each area and how each relates to the surrounding areas. Georgina had old, dull skin with layers of dead keratinocytes and slow skin turnover on the outside. She had lines around her eyes, across her forehead and down her cheeks, lips and lower face. She had fat pad loss around her temples, cheeks and chin. In short, she had facial attributes that made her look tired and sad. Fixing her mid and lower face, I would be able to restore her to her old self.

Strategy

My initial design was to start Georgina with fillers in the most affected areas: her cheeks and tear troughs. I planned to begin in her midface and then work my way down to her lips and lower face. I also considered treating her with Botox to relax her muscles, improve her lines and lift her eyes. Fillers in her skin would not be enough, as clearly evidenced by the deep lines down the sides of her cheeks. I would need to stimulate her collagen through microneedling, skin peels and my favourite restoration treatment, Profhilo (see

Chapter 14). Before starting, I discussed this strategy with Georgina, including the risks, cost and time frame.

Shape

Georgina's restoration took several months for multiple reasons. She had fibromyalgia, which makes the injections more painful than usual, and she bruises more easily, the bruising taking longer to clear. These problems caused her to relapse emotionally. Some days when she came to the clinic looking unhappy, I would just make her a cup of tea and, instead, focus on her skin, prescribing treatments that would continue to transform her without being so invasive.

Skin

With an effective skin treatment, Georgina was thriving. We had finally reached the top of Maslow's Hierarchy, and Georgina was the woman she wanted to be. Or was she?

It was not long before she had another setback and I saw the old Georgina starting to emerge again. Her muscles were flabby, her movements less fluid, her skin was dull and her hair not its usual mane of shiny gold locks. What was happening? That's when it dawned on me that we had addressed her external needs but not her internal needs. Georgina still had aches and pains, brain fog, tiredness, emotional lows, forgetfulness, bloating, fluctuating weight despite exercise, and loneliness. Her relationship with her partner had broken down, and she was single again.

These ongoing problems were affecting her ageing significantly. No amount of filler or skincare would help Georgina, and we needed to adopt a different approach. I didn't want to keep filling her face with filler and toxins when we hadn't looked at her hormones.

Supplement

Georgina represents my typical patient over the age of forty-five who is experiencing symptoms of menopause. She was fifty-seven and had not had any treatment to replace her hormones. Due to her pains and emotional setbacks, I knew that she would not be eating well or regularly, and certainly not supplementing. Whatever I did outwardly, her hormones and nutrition would continue to 'age' her.

I did a blood test and found that her blood was deficient in DHEA, oestrogen, testosterone and progesterone. No wonder she was feeling and looking so tired. We then started Georgina on bioidentical hormones, and within three months she was thriving on the inside and outside. Her skin and hair had improved, her brain fog had cleared, she had no more pain and was feeling happy within herself. She was looking forward to each day with renewed energy and excitement. Georgina now cares about her hormones more than any skin treatment.

Sustain

Georgina continued to have treatment for the next five years. Her restoration journey continued with improvements to her cheeks and eyes using Botox and fillers. We then had to restore her collagen by applying the 5C

Skincare Programme, which consisted of cosmeceutical skincare, microneedling, vampire technique and Profhilo treatments. In between she had some beautification with lip and brow treatments. The picture was completed by supplementing her hormones and therefore nourishing Georgina from the inside out.

Georgina looking nourished and renewed

Summary

Taking care of your skin should be part of a holistic, total-body programme that assesses your individual journey through life and your unique physical and emotional needs: what I call the 7S Process for Agelessness: Story, Structure, Strategy, Shape, Supplement, Skin, Sustain.

14

Complementary Treatments For Cell Regeneration

As we learned in the previous chapter, maintaining excellent outcomes sometimes involves looking beyond Botox and filler at complementary treatments. These include skin peels, mesotherapy, microneedling, injectable platelet-rich fibrin (IPRF or so-called vampire facials) and my favourite treatment, Profhilo. These treatments further support collagen regeneration, improving skin texture and integrity, but above all they are more affordable and help to sustain and improve your outcomes. When patients are not keen on injectables (fillers) and toxins (Botox), this is the first port of call and is less invasive and therefore less intimidating. These treatments are also seen as green because they are more natural.

Skin peels

Skin peels, also called chemical peels, are the third most commonly performed noninvasive cosmetic procedure, after botulinum toxins and soft tissue fillers.[43] As its name suggests, a chemical peel is a treatment where a chemical is applied to the skin and allowed to soak in. This process destroys parts of the skin in a controlled way so that new skin can grow in its place. This both loosens the old, dead skin and changes the pH of the skin. The result is a more even, luminescent skin tone and texture. Chemical peels increase skin turnover and make more fibroblasts, which will make more collagen.

Skin peels are one of the most misunderstood procedures, and their value is underappreciated. The reason for this is the name – patients frequently ask me if the skin will be hanging from their face. The second reason patients are concerned about skin peels is because we use acids to change the skin, which feels counterintuitive as acids ordinarily cause harm. The key thing to remember is that these chemicals are used in a highly controlled way.

The acid level in a chemical peel is adjusted according to the pH of your skin: the lower the number of a peel, the stronger the acid. For instance, 1 is far stronger than 6. The stronger the acid, the deeper its penetration – superficial, medium or deep. Small changes in acid levels can make huge changes in the skin, so expertise is essential on the part of the practitioner.

A skin peel creates an 'injury' at a specific depth in the skin to stimulate new skin growth and improve the surface texture and appearance. It removes dead skin at the surface and stimulates epidermal growth and collagen renewal. Skin peels also whiten sun-damaged skin. They level out melanin distribution, decreasing discolouration and hyperpigmentation, and remove abnormalities in dry skin. They also produce GAGs and hyaluronic acid in the skin layers, improving dermal hydration and thickness. The result is younger-looking skin with a smoother texture and increased blood flow. Skin peels help produce healthy, glowing skin with reduced pigment and fine lines and wrinkles.

I value skin peels highly in practice and like to use them before patients start their skincare regime, as they ensure that the products are better absorbed and have quicker results. Regular peels are also beneficial in supporting ongoing improvement.

Potential side effects

The deeper the peel, the more significant the change in the skin and the higher the risk of complications. Peels of superficial to medium depth are safe and generally well tolerated but can cause mild discomfort during the procedure. After a deep peel, you might want to avoid being seen for a few days, as your skin might look as if it has been sunburned, but this settles quickly. You might also experience a slight burning sensation and irritation, but this is normally also transient. Scarring from skin peels is rare, and it is nonexistent with superficial peels.

Certain peels are not advised in dark skin because they can cause pigmentary changes known as post-inflammatory hyperpigmentation. Deeper peels can cause infection or improper healing, especially if you pick at the dead skin, resulting in scarring. Acne eruptions can occur but are easily treatable. Sunscreen is a must after any skin peel, regularly applied and adequately spread over the skin. To minimise the risk of side effects, it is vital that the practitioner understands your needs and skin type.

Microneedling

Microneedling is a procedure where the surface of the skin is punctured using fine needles. It is also known as percutaneous collagen induction. The procedure is minimally invasive and uses various devices at different depths. The instruments used are a derma roller, a derma stamp and my favourite, a derma pen: a rapid electronic puncturing device with adjustable needle depth and speed. The needles penetrate the skin up to 3 mm deep and when performing several passes over an area create up to 83,000 holes per minute, depending on the device used. The depth of the needles is adjustable according to the different skin: for instance, the fine thin skin under the eye compared to the thicker skin on the chin and cheek.

This 'controlled injury' within the skin triggers fibroblasts, which signal growth factors to the damaged area, where collagen and elastin are produced to close the wound and generate new skin. The treatment improves skin quality and appearance, especially for fine lines and wrinkles, and is also excellent for scars, hair loss and stretch marks.

Mesotherapy

Mesotherapy is a treatment in which a bespoke cocktail of powerful vitamins, essential amino acids, minerals and antioxidants is injected into the lower layers of the skin using a meso device with one needle. This is in contrast to microneedling, which punctures the surface skin. The purpose of mesotherapy is to improve dull, tired skin and superficial wrinkles. It also aids circulation, improving overall skin texture, and evens out pigment, resulting in a healthy glow.

Although microneedling appears more robust and effective in practice, I like to combine the two methods: first injecting the 'cocktail' of products, then needling the skin and finally flooding the tissue with products again.

Mesotherapy can be combined with filler treatments: a light dermafiller is injected superficially under the skin around the eyes or mouth before a soft, malleable filler is used to improve skin texture and eliminate fine lines and wrinkles.

Vampire facials

'Vampire facial' is a term commonly used to describe a treatment in which your own blood is used to revitalise your skin. The procedure also goes by several other names, the best-known being IPRP or IPRF. IPRF is the newest kid on the block and a development of IPRP; there are slight differences to how the blood is treated.[44]

The term 'vampire facial' sounds intimidating but it is in effect an extension of the body's amazing capacity to heal itself. Our blood is rich in growth factors (platelets) that can provide enormous benefits to our skin. Platelets play a key role in maintaining the integrity of cell walls, as well as repairing defects caused by injury. During a controlled injury such as microneedling, platelets multiply to repair the cell wall, forming collagen and elastin.

We perform the vampire technique by drawing your blood into a tube, then putting it through a centrifuge, separating the plasma from the blood. The plasma is then extracted with a needle and either reinjected or needled back into the skin, wound, hair or wherever there is a need to signal growth factors and produce collagen for repair.

It is a process that blends science, physiology and advanced aesthetic techniques to improve the quality of your skin in significant ways. The treatment helps your skin to function optimally by hydrating it and increasing blood flow and collagen production, essential to radiant and healthy-looking skin.

Microneedling and vampire facials stimulate collagen production near the surface, and cosmeceutical skincare will even texture, colour and tone. We also needed something that would regenerate and moisturise the deeper tissues. One such product is the phenomenal Profhilo.

Profhilo

Profhilo is one of the most magical products I have had the pleasure to use. The manufacturers advertise it as revolutionary treatment, and I agree. Profhilo yields results in the lower face that are comparable to what Botox does for the upper face. It is extremely popular among my patients and surpasses the sales of Botox and fillers. The uniqueness of Profhilo is that it has the ability to enhance collagen and elastin formation and stem cell viability in the skin, making it an excellent restorative product. As already discussed throughout this book, our collagen and elastin fibre structure change with ageing. Profhilo addresses both these aspects, which conventional treatments have not been able to accomplish.

Profhilo contains a form of hyaluronic acid that is produced in a different way from traditional methods, allowing the hyaluronic acid to disperse evenly throughout the skin to produce more collagen and elastin, transforming tired, dull-looking skin into firm, juicy and luminous skin. While traditional dermal fillers also contain hyaluronic acid, the key difference between the two treatments is that Profhilo doesn't add volume or change the structure of the face. Hyaluronic acid in fillers stays in a single place to create volume, while the thinner hyaluronic acid in Profhilo spreads evenly across the skin. Profhilo can be used in conjunction with dermal fillers to add volume and structure while improving the overall quality of the skin.

The injections are in five areas on each side of the face, using a specific technique developed for Profhilo known as bio-aesthetic point. When injected, it makes you look as if you have been stung by a bee. It slowly spreads like a thick gloop of honey under the skin in a 5 cm radius and starts to hydrate the skin in the hours that follow. Over the next few weeks, collagen and elastin production is stimulated, producing a secondary effect of skin tightening. This is useful because levels of collagen, elastin and hyaluronic acid in the skin rapidly drop from the age of thirty, resulting in signs of ageing such as fine lines, wrinkles and lacklustre skin. Profhilo acts to reverse some of these changes.

One more treatment is required a month later and, for most patients, further treatments every six months to ensure adequate hydration and collagen regeneration. If the skin is severely dehydrated, more treatments are advisable. The maximum effect of Profhilo is usually seen two months after the second treatment.

The 'best' treatment

There is no 'silver bullet' in aesthetic medicine; no single treatment can fix all your problems and maintain the results you want. No treatment will yield the same results in every patient, since anatomically we are all unique. Each of the methods I have described in this book has a role to play in making you age less – and ultimately ageless.

Which you choose will, of course, depend partly on cost – not only how much you can afford, but also how much you think you are worth. You will naturally want to shop around and, in doing so, you should be aware of several things.

First, as we have seen, what you think you need (Botox, filler, etc) may not be what you really need in terms of addressing the anatomical, hormonal and nutritional changes that have caused the effects you see when you look in the mirror. Only a highly qualified, experienced practitioner will be able to assess your real needs accurately and precisely.

The 'best' practice

As we have also seen, not all aestheticians are equal. The industry is unregulated, which means that anyone can offer 'aesthetic services'. Aesthetics is also a matter of taste, and what one person views as beautiful is horrifying to another.

There is also a question of safety. Things can go wrong even for the most experienced practitioner. A severe (but fortunately rare) adverse reaction to filler injections, for example, is vascular occlusion. If left untreated, the loss of blood supply will cause the surrounding tissue to die. Fillers can also occlude arteries and stop blood flow, resulting in tissue death and even blindness. In extreme cases, treatment can cause stroke or death. There are many possible reasons for this, other than pure incompetence, including how products have been stored, the patient's metabolism, and whether the patient accurately describes their medical condition before treatment and follows the aftercare advice.

What is important is how the practitioner deals with such problems. Most of them can be reversed, but your practitioner needs to know what to do. If they don't, or if they don't respond soon enough, you can be literally scarred for life. It is crucial to have easy access to your injector. If your injector is not local to you and something goes wrong, what then?

When choosing a practitioner, one of the best places to look is Save Face.[45] Save Face offers independent information about nonsurgical cosmetic treatments. The website enables you to search, compare and rate Save Face-accredited practitioners throughout the UK. This saves you time and gives you confidence that the provider has met the standards you should expect. Save Face ensures standards of practice in an unregulated world and will carry out an investigation on your behalf if you have an adverse event. Even if nothing goes wrong, it is essential that your practitioner provides you with more than just 'treatment'. You are entitled to a Process of Care, which involves four stages.

First, you should be given time and opportunity to give your full story, which is why you meet with your practitioner. Once every part of that story is properly understood, with all the associated previous history and medical problems, and you are satisfied that your needs have been fully assessed, a treatment plan is devised. The treatment plan is based on the best available evidence and knowledge at that time. The treatment is then carried out in accordance with that plan. The last step, the review, is one of the most crucial and that is to assess whether the plan has worked. At this stage, you and your practitioner critically analyse your results and whether the treatment has met your expectations. You might then decide to have further treatment, which means that the process should be repeated: meet, plan, treat and review.

This model should be at the core of any aesthetic business or where patients are concerned as it ensures continuity of care. Practices where clinicians 'fly in' (sometimes literally) to deliver treatments cannot meet this requirement. The optimum results of a treatment may not be obtained until weeks or even months afterwards. Your plan should always include a follow-up appointment with your practitioner at the appropriate time to review your treatment.

Summary

When choosing a practitioner, here are the questions to ask:

- Are they suitably qualified and experienced and Save Face-accredited?

- Do you know about and trust the products that they are going to put in your face?

- Does the practitioner understand all the risks involved, and will they explain these to you?

- Will you be asked to sign a consent form and given aftercare leaflets?

- Are they readily available in case things go wrong?

- Are you confident that they can resolve and treat you if things do go wrong?

- Will you be given a full review of your treatment at the appropriate time?

Whatever your outcomes, you deserve the best. It is your body and your life that are at stake.

Conclusion

There is a moral case for treating and preventing ageing because it is not about enabling people to live longer but helping them to live happier and more fulfilled lives, free from disease. Ageing is a disease and not a fact of life; as such, it can be treated, and our lives can be enhanced as a result. The common acceptance that we should 'grow old gracefully' is senseless, now that there is so much we can do, thanks to science and technology, to counter the effects of ageing and keep ourselves ageless.

When it comes to treating the human body, the whole is so much greater than the sum of its parts. Think of the body as a symphony orchestra: the music it makes is so much more beautiful when all the players are in tune with each other. Our body comprises a mass of parts that must work together in synchrony to ensure our survival and wellbeing. If any one of those parts malfunctions, the impact resonates throughout our body, causing injury, illness and ageing.

We don't have a manual to follow or a bank of red lights that illuminate when something isn't working correctly. Our experience of things going wrong is also subjective and difficult to describe. It can take a long time for things that go wrong to show their impact on our health. In many cases, we are not actually ill, but neither are we well, and it is unfair to expect our GPs and conventional medicine to provide the answer.

More than ever before, we need to take responsibility for our own wellbeing and understand that we are in charge of our bodies, and that what we put into them and how we treat them will have long-term consequences. At the same time, we need to realise that we are unique, and what works for others will not necessarily work for us. When it comes to treatment, one size definitely does not fit all.

Aesthetic medicine is an exciting new field in the move towards agelessness, and it is now more mainstream than ever, but we can do so much more. There are many ways to biohack your body to reduce the damage done to it and reduce ageing at the cellular level. Blood tests, DNA analyses and nutrigenomics are all ways to find out how well your body is working – whether all its parts are in synch and, if not, what to do about it. Treatments such as nutraceuticals, bioidentical hormones, cosmeceuticals, regenerative therapies and aesthetic treatments address both the inside and the outside of your body, working together to achieve the optimum outcomes.

Nothing is as personal as understanding your DNA and how your body is organised to reprogramme, reproduce and survive. Cellular injury occurs due to injury, illness and disease, including metabolic processes in your body. We require energy to survive, and we get this energy from our muscles and food. If the vitamins, minerals and amino acids are not available in our body's cellular process, it will scavenge them from elsewhere, rapidly depleting our DNA pool, leading to ageing. Our hormones also change with age, further affecting our body function. Accurate testing results in precision treatments to minimise the injury and ageing effects on our internal cellular structure.

The ravages of life also create havoc on the outside of our body, affecting bone, fat pads, muscles and skin. Different treatment modalities are available to effectively treat the outer body, reversing the visible signs of ageing. Choosing suitable treatments and practitioners is challenging due to market noise and poor regulation. This book has helped you navigate this minefield and find your own personal path through it.

Investing in your health and wellbeing is the best gift you can give to yourself. You no longer need to accept the status quo. Ageing is no longer a fact of life; it is a choice. Agelessness is achievable. You only have one life; make it the best you can.

Notes

1 S Bulterijs et al (2015) 'It is time to classify biological aging as a disease', *Frontiers in Genetics*, 6, www.frontiersin.org/article/10.3389/fgene.2015.00205, accessed 25 February 2022

2 C López-Otín et al (2013) 'The hallmarks of aging', *Cell*, 153/6, pp1194–1217, www.cell.com/cell/fulltext/S0092-8674(13)00645-4, accessed 25 February 2022

3 DA Sinclair (2019) *Lifespan: Why we age – and why we don't have to*, New York: HarperCollins

4 AH Maslow (1943) 'A theory of human motivation', *Psychological Review*, 50, pp370–396, available at: Research History (2012) 'Maslow's Hierarchy of Needs', www.researchhistory.org/2012/06/16/maslows-hierarchy-of-needs, accessed 8 February 2022

5 T Şimşek, HU Şimşek and NZ Cantürk (2014) 'Response to trauma and metabolic changes: Posttraumatic metabolism', *Turkish Journal of Surgery*, volume 30(3) pp153–159

6 TY Kim et al (1997) 'The effect of trauma and PTSD on telomere length: An exploratory study in people exposed to combat trauma', *Scientific Reports*, volume 7, www.nature.com/articles/s41598–017–04682-w, accessed 4 November 2021

7 A Steele (2020) *Ageless: The new science of getting older without getting old*, London: Bloomsbury

8 The Global Wellness Institute (2020) 'What is the wellness economy?', https://globalwellnessinstitute.org/what-is-wellness/what-is-the-wellness-economy, accessed 9 February 2022

9 The Global Wellness Institute (2021) *The Global Wellness Trends Report: The future of wellness 2021*, https://globalwellnessinstitute.org/global-wellness-institute-blog/2020/12/29/global-wellness-trends-report-the-future-of-wellness-2021, accessed 27 January 2022

10 See note 8.

11 Centre for Ageing Better (no date) 'Ageing population', https://ageing-better.org.uk, accessed 31 January 2022

12 By the Danish physiologist Christian Bohr, hence known as the Bohr effect: A Benner et al (2022) 'Physiology, Bohr effect', *StatPearls*, https://pubmed.ncbi.nlm.nih.gov/30252284, accessed 8 February 2022

13 R Kurzweil and T Grossman (2005) *Fantastic Voyage: Live long enough to live forever: The science behind radical life extension*, New York: Penguin

14 AE Clarke et al (2003) 'Biomedicalization: Technoscientific transformations of health, illness, and U.S. biomedicine', *American Sociological Review*, 68(2), pp161–194

15 See footnote 10

16 See footnote 10

17 D Mozaffarian, I Rosenberg and R Uauy (2018) 'History of modern nutrition science: Implications for current research, dietary guidelines, and food policy', *BMJ*, 361, k2392, https://bmj.com/content/361/bmj.k2392, accessed 31 January 2022

18 IntraVita (no date) 'IV drips and booster shots', www.intravitamedical.com, accessed 25 February 2022

19 T Malan (2018) 'Nutraceuticals – snake oil or real medicine?', *ResearchGate*, www.researchgate.net/publication/341158975_Nutraceuticals_-_Snake_Oil_or_Real_Medicine, accessed 25 February 2022

20 Grand View Research (2021) *Dietary Supplements Market Size, Share and Trends Analysis Report by Ingredient (Vitamins, Proteins and Amino Acids), by Form, by Application, by End User, by Distribution Channel, and Segment Forecasts, 2021–2028*, www.grandviewresearch.com/industry-analysis/dietary-supplements-market, accessed 31 January 2022

21 Remember, antioxidants protect us from free radicals by restoring electrons throughout the body (see Chapter 2).

22 R Kurzweil and T Grossman (2005) *Fantastic Voyage: Live long enough to live forever: The science behind radical life extension*, New York: Penguin Group

23 P Stute et al (2016) 'A model of care for healthy menopause and ageing: EMAS position statement', *Maturitas*, 92, pp1–6

24 E Laumann et al (2005) 'Sexual problems among women and men aged 40–80y: Prevalence and correlates identified

in the Global Study of Sexual Attitudes and Behaviors', *International Journal of Impotence Research*, 17(1), pp39–57

25 S Somers (2007) *Ageless: The Naked Truth about Bioidentical Hormones*. New York: Harmony

26 O Svejme et al (2012) 'Early menopause and risk of osteoporosis, fracture and mortality: A 34-year prospective observational study in 390 women', *An International Journal of Obstetrics and Gynaecology*, 119(7), pp810–816

27 The Marion Gluck Clinic (2021) 'Feel like yourself again with the help of Hormone Balancing Therapy', www.mariongluckclinic.com, accessed 31 January 2022

28 Our thyroid regulates everything from our breathing and heart rate to our muscle strength and body temperature. Our thyroid also produces several hormones that are crucial to our growth, development and good health.

29 F Labrie and C Labrie (2013) 'DHEA and intracrinology at menopause, a positive choice for evolution of the human species', *Climacteric*, 16, pp205–213; M Holton, C Thorne and AT Goldstein (2020) 'An overview of dehydroepiandrosterone (EM-760) as a treatment option for genitourinary syndrome of menopause', *Expert Opinion on Pharmacotherapy*, 21:4, pp409–415; R Kurzweil and T Grossman (2005) *A Fantastic Voyage: Live long enough to live forever*, New York: Plume Book

30 H Lambers et al (2006) 'Natural skin surface pH is on average below 5, which is beneficial for its resident flora', *International Journal of Cosmetic Science*, 28(5), pp359–370

31 Statista (2020) 'Cosmetics market in the United Kingdom: Statistics and facts', www.statista.com/topics/5760/cosmetics-market-in-the-united-kingdom-uk, accessed 1 February 2022

32 Grand View Research (2022) *Non-invasive Aesthetic Treatment Market Size, Share and Trends Analysis Report by Procedure (Skin Rejuvenation, Injectable), by End Use (Hospital/Surgery Center, MedSpa), by Region, and Segment Forecasts, 2022–2030*, www.grandviewresearch.com/industry-analysis/non-invasive-aesthetic-treatment-market, accessed 1 February 2022

33 BAAPS (British Association of Aesthetic Plastic Surgeons) (2019) 'Plastic surgery: It's not teens, it's their grandparents!

British association of aesthetic plastic surgeons reveal age trends', https://baaps.org.uk/media/press_releases/1273/plastic_surgery_its_not_teens_its_their_grandparents, accessed 31 January 2022

34   D Diaz (2012) 'Minors and cosmetic surgery: An argument for state intervention', *DePaul Journal of Health Care Law*, 14(2), pp236–269

35   A Ouellette (2012) 'Body modification and adolescent decision making: Proceed with caution', *Journal of Health Care Law and Policy*, 15(1), pp120–152

36   E Chang (2019) 'Taking the mystery out of Botox and dermal fillers', American Society of Plastic Surgeons, www.plasticsurgery.org/news/blog/taking-the-mystery-out-of-botox-and-dermal-fillers, accessed 1 February 2022

37   P Ting and A Freiman (2004) 'The story of *Clostridium botulinum*: From food poisoning to Botox', *Clinical Medicine*, 4(3), pp258–261, https://pubmed.ncbi.nlm.nih.gov/15244362, accessed 25 February 2022

38   J Kablik et al (2009) 'Comparative physical properties of hyaluronic acid dermal fillers', *Dermatologic Surgery*, 35, pp30–312, https://doi.org/10.1111/j.1524-4725.2008.01046.x, accessed 25 February 2022

39   O Jones and B Selinger (2021) 'The chemistry of cosmetics', www.science.org.au/curious/people-medicine/chemistry-cosmetics, accessed 31 January 2022

40   A A O'Connor et al (2018) 'Chemical peels: A review of current practice', *Australasian Journal of Dermatology*, 59, pp171–181, https://onlinelibrary.wiley.com/doi/pdf/10.1111/ajd.12715, accessed 31 January 2022

41   K Becker, 'This dermatologist thinks you should give up moisturizer forever', *Refinery29*, www.refinery29.com/en-us/is-moisturizer-bad-for-you, accessed 25 February 2022

42   A photon is a particle representing a quantum of light or other electromagnetic radiation.

43   T Soleymani (2018) 'A practical approach to chemical peels: A review of fundamentals and step-by-step algorithmic protocol for treatment', *Journal of Clinical and Aesthetic Dermatology*, volume 11(8) pp21–28

44 In a study I performed with my colleagues, we concluded
    that IPRF has higher amounts of growth factors and
    should therefore have a better impact in terms of hair
    and skin regeneration: T Malan (2020) 'Comparative
    study of platelet count: injectable platelet rich fibrin (i-prf)
    compared to platelet rich plasma (PRP): Controlled in vitro
    laboratory study', ResearchGate, www.researchgate.net/
    publication/339712298_Comparative_Study_of_Platelet_
    Count_Injectable_Platelet_Rich_Fibrin_i-PRF_Compared_
    to_Platelet_Rich_Plasma_PRP_-Controlled_in_vitro_
    laboratory_study, accessed 7 February 2022

45 www.saveface.co.uk

Acknowledgements

My journey in writing this book started with the indomitable and amazing Daniel Priestley and the Dent Team, including my accountability group, Lee Evans, Antoinette Daniels, Stephen Walsh, Giuseppe Marzio and the many others who pushed me out of my comfort zone. I know I haven't listed you all, but please know I thank you from the bottom of my heart. I also thank Fluid Ideas, the creative, branding and marketing team behind my ideas and aspirations, who are always on hand when I need to get concepts clear and out into the world – especially the amazing Gail Hodson Walker, brand ambassador and infographic creator, who brings my business to life. I must also thank my amazing colleagues Ginny and Danielle, who supported me every step of the way when I was hunkered behind my desk, ensuring that the clinic continued to tick over.

My beta readers, Melanie Benham, Lindsey Wallace, Tim Norfolk and Sabrina Shah-Desai, you have been magnificent in your feedback and encouragement. Lindsey Wallace, you need a special mention for having been my mentor for so long and for encouraging me to jump out of my comfort zone and into self-employment and entrepreneurship. I must also give thanks and praise to Lucy McCarraher and Joe Gregory at Rethink Press for focusing my thoughts. The person who must have suffered the most is my amazing editor, Joe Laredo, who challenged and questioned me every step of the way, coaxing me to produce a much better and easier read than the one I gave him at first. Your patience and kindness have been fantastic and much appreciated.

A special dedication to my parents, Franz and Yvonne, who taught us sisters to dream big, show no fear and live life to the full. In particular, my mum, who sadly passed away during the writing of this book. She taught me love, care, compassion and encouraged me into nursing. Special thanks to my amazing husband, David Malan (the ball catcher), who cheers me on from the sidelines, who patiently cooked, cleaned and supported me throughout the process. You are one of the best.

Thank you to so many people who have touched my life and on whose shoulders I stand now – the big influencers in this fascinating tapestry of life. The list is incredibly long, but the majority of you know who you are. Special thanks to every patient; you remain my teachers and inspire me the most. I love you all.

Finally, thank you to so many friends, colleagues and patients, you have been my mentors, influencers, inspirations, tutors and fellow travellers. God bless you and grant you happy travels in this journey we call life. May you all remain ageless, healthy and happy.

The Author

Tania Malan is Founder and Clinician Director of Uniskin Wellness Clinic. She has thirty years' experience in trauma and medicine in South Africa and the United Kingdom. An eternal student, she has four degrees, three of them at master's level, as well as diplomas in midwifery, psychiatry and general and community nursing. She has written over twenty-five research papers and several publications and developed programmes in advanced practice. She is a visiting lecturer on advanced practice at Nottingham Medical School and Derby University.

Tania has a passion for the human body and enjoys understanding its inner workings and anatomy and how it responds to disease – above all its ability to heal and care for itself. Deep down she is a healer and a carer, and she flourishes when she is able to support people to live their best lives. She also has a deep appreciation of what it is to live well and strives to support everyone to achieve just that – to enjoy balance, hope and agelessness.

🌐 www.uniskin.co.uk

⬜ www.facebook.com/UniSkinUK

Lightning Source UK Ltd.
Milton Keynes UK
UKHW020838030622
403929UK00005B/148

9 781781 336779